# WHAT OTHERS ARE SAYING

Once in a lifetime you meet someone who changes your paradigm not necessarily by what they say, but rather by the actions of their life. When I met Dr Lonnie Rex instantly it was obvious that he was a man of great stature and his shadow had stretched over the continents of the world. His life reflects that he has carried the enormous burden of caring for the hurting and the suffering in the world. What an inspiration this book will be to every reader! The stories found here are awe inspiring as well as encouraging that every person can reach a higher potential than they ever thought possible. Read about the high dramas of danger, political intrigue and Christian love that have been shared in many areas from the heights of various governments to the depths of humanity. You are about to embark on one of the greatest books you will ever read!

—Dr Gayla Holly

# MY AMAZING ADVENTURES WITH GOD

*Dr. Lonnie Rex with
Richard Young*

# MY AMAZING
# ADVENTURES
# WITH GOD

## FROM POLIO AND
## PARALYSIS TO
## WALKING WITH
## THE POPE

WINTERS
PUBLISHING GROUP

Published by Winters Publishing, LLC
2448 E. 81st St. Suite #4802 | Tulsa, Oklahoma 74137 USA

Book design copyright © 2013 by Winters Publishing, LLC. All rights reserved.
*Cover design by Joel Uber*
*Interior design by Mary Jean Archival*

Published in the United States of America

ISBN: 978-1-62902-938-2
Biography & Autobiography / Personal Memoirs
13.10.25

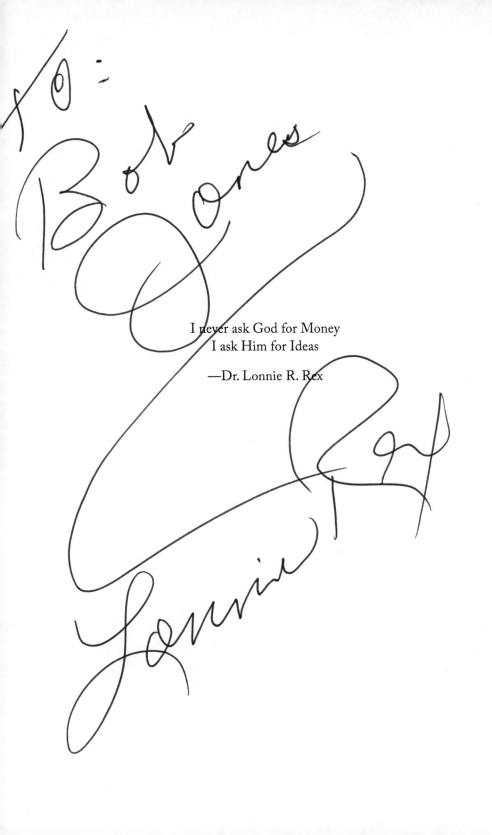

I never ask God for Money
I ask Him for Ideas

—Dr. Lonnie R. Rex

# DEDICATION

This book is dedicated to Betty, my wife of 64 years. She has traveled the world with me. She gave a mother's love to children in 25 orphanages. She loved lepers isolated in remote colonies in countries around the world. Together we played piano duet concerts entertaining presidents, preachers, prime ministers and paupers.

I would also like to dedicate this to our three children; Royce, Patricia, and Debbie. I missed so much of their lives being away for long periods of time. Also to my staff of 60, they made it possible to carry on, raise funds, and correspond with the faithful donors who made it all possible for thirty years.

God Bless All of You.

—Lonnie R. Rex

# WORDS FROM A LOVING WIFE

My dear husband was stricken with polio in 1937 when he was nine. He spent over a year of his childhood in the Oklahoma Children's Hospital for several operations. He wore leg braces until college. Even with one leg short than the other and limping in pain, he touched the world. He led international ministries and humanitarian organizations that supported orphanages, jungle hospitals and leper colonies. As his wife it has been my joy to be by his side visiting the many projects around the world. It has been an amazing adventure with God and my husband, Lonnie Rex.

God Bless.

—Betty Rex

# FOREWORD

Dr. Lonnie R. Rex is the son of a Pentecostal Holiness preacher who became the executive director of Evangelism and World Missions for the denomination. As a child Lonnie was stricken with polio. His life was in the balance. He was not expected to live. His parents' prayers touched the heart of God to spare his life. He overcame this physical challenge miraculously.

Through his father's preaching, Lonnie's heart was captured by the story of the lad who gave his lunch of five barley loaves and two small fish to Jesus. That became Lonnie's burning desire to give what he had to Jesus. It became the motivating force in the extensive ministries God gave him. Lonnie never asked anything from God for himself. He prayed that God would give him ideas, concepts, and wisdom to help others. God answered his prayer.

For many years Lonnie served well-known American evangelists. God gifted Lonnie to be one of the foremost fundraisers of the 20th Century through letter writing that funded the costs of mass evangelism and healing ministries. His writing style touched the hearts of people to give generously, and God blessed his effort to help others through these various ministries.

God led Lonnie to create the David Livingstone Foundation. It brought food, clothing, shelter, and education, as well as financial, medical and spiritual resources to many nations. He sent boats to carry hundreds of Vietnamese refugees to safety. He provided ambulances, built clinics, hospitals, and orphanages on three continents. As you read this book of intriguing stories

Lonnie tells of the challenges and opportunities to help needy people. You will discover what a man endowed with a generous heart and committed to God can do to serve humanity.

I met Lonnie Rex in 1954 when I was playing trombone in the Quantico Marine Band for President Eisenhower. We met at the National Pentecostal Holiness Church in Washington, DC. That friendship has endured. I consider Lonnie a treasured and trusted friend.

*Dr. Hugh H. Morgan*

Dr. Hugh H. Morgan is an ordained minister with the IPHC. He has served as a pastor, Air Force chaplain, and college president. He was elected chairman of the National Association of Evangelicals. He is former president of Southwestern College, now Southwestern Christian University. He is the founder and editor of Hugh's News, Inc. It has a website and a newsletter with over 6,000 readers worldwide. His website is: www.hughsnews.com.

# INTRODUCTION

Talking to Lonnie Rex for the first time is something I will never forget. It was one of those moments that will stay in your mind for the rest of your life. I remember hearing about the assassinations of John and Robert Kennedy, Dr. King, and the crash of Challenger. I remember when man landed on the moon. I remember talking with Lonnie Rex for the first time. Something inside says life is about to become different. That voice was right. More right than I could have ever imagined.

One Sunday night, Brenda and I had met our friend Tom Nix at our favorite Tex-Mex place. This is one of those places where the waitress recognizes us when we walked inside. She knows what soft drinks to bring to the table without asking. She even knows what appetizer to bring before we look at menus. Tom is the type of friend you may not see for a few weeks at a time, but when you get together, it is like you see each other every day. We were catching up on what projects we were doing. Brenda is a sculptress. She is always doing something new. Tom is a very talented musician with a marvelous voice and concert quality keyboard skills. In that company, there is no question I am the least talented.

I had just finished sending my latest book to the publisher. Tom asked what my next project would be. I mentioned a few possibilities, and gave the pros and cons of each. Tom provided some input on the various options. Suddenly, it was like a light switched on inside of his head. You could almost see the light bulb above him. Tom said to me, "You should write a book about my friend Lonnie Rex!"

I had heard of the late R.L. Rex. He had served as the director of Foreign Missions for the International Pentecostal Holiness Church for over thirty years. But I had never heard of Lonnie Rex. So I asked, "Who is Lonnie Rex?"

Tom was almost leaping out of his seat as he gestured and talked. His enthusiasm was very contagious. I looked around to see if we were drawing the attention of everyone in the restaurant. "Lonnie Rex is just the most amazing man you will ever meet in your life! He has met everyone in the world from Pope John Paul II to Mohammed Ali to Mikhail Gorbachev. He has worked with Oral Roberts and TL Osborn. He led his own charity where he took food, medicine, and equipment to people all over the world. He knows George and Barbara Bush! He is the most connected man in Christianity! He knows everybody. He's just the most unbelievable guy ever!"

At this point I didn't know whether to believe him or not. I didn't question Tom's honesty, but the whole thing sounded incredible. Tom continued to talk with great gusto about this man I had never heard of. He described going to their house in Tulsa, when he was in college. Lonnie had a daughter Tom's age, and they had been great friends. He mentioned the huge house they had at Southern Hills Country Club in Tulsa. He talked about the beautiful art they had. He told us how he and Lonnie's daughter were stopped driving a Rolls Royce that belonged to Lonnie. The police were questioning two college students driving such a luxurious car. It took a phone call to Lonnie to prove it was legit. He seemed to talk forever. Every story was more outlandish than the one before.

I was almost overwhelmed. If the things he said were true, I wasn't sure about meeting him. But even if he was stretching the truth, this guy seemed to be very interesting. But I was sure there had to be more to the story than I was hearing. Suddenly, Tom said something that grabbed my immediate attention. "Let's give Lonnie a call!"

That totally caught me off guard. First, I had never heard of this guy before tonight. Second, it was well after ten o'clock on a Sunday night. Third, he had told me that Lonnie was in his seventies! I don't know any man that age who likes getting phone calls at nearly eleven o'clock on a Sunday night. Finally, I really wanted to know more about him, before I talked to him in person! I'm the kind of guy who likes to do the research, before I dive into something. If Lonnie had done everything Tom said, there had to be some things on the internet to confirm at least some of this. But Tom wasn't hearing anything I had to say. Before I knew it, Tom had his phone out of his pocket and began to dial. Suddenly I heard Tom say, "Miss Betty! How are you? It is so good to hear your voice, Sweetheart. Is Lonnie around? Can I talk with him?"

My heart began to race. I shouldn't say it, but I do like control when I am writing. But I heard Tom talking, and I knew I had no control whatsoever. "Brother Lonnie! How are you doing? Listen I am here eating with my good friends Rick and Brenda Young. Rick is the famous author Richard Young, you might have heard about him." Tom was laying it on thick. "He is looking for another book project, and I told him about you. Why don't you talk to him? Here Rick, talk to Lonnie."

I found myself taking his phone and talking to a stranger. But I spoke to him like an old friend. "Brother Lonnie, how are you?" We spoke to each other for a couple of minutes. In that short time, he talked of the Pope, Gorbachev, and Oral Roberts. He mentioned working with Mohammed Ali, and meeting Winston Churchill. He talked of traveling the world, and meeting with kings and presidents. He mentioned being arrested in Africa. He talked of taking food and medicine everywhere through his charity. Lonnie talked of building schools and hospitals. I was still amazed. The story was getting bigger and bigger.

After a few minutes of conversation, I handed Tom back his phone. I expected Tom to say goodbye, and that be the end of it. No, not Tom, he was determined to get Lonnie and I together. My head was swimming with the phone conversation I had just had. Suddenly, I heard Tom inviting us to visit these people I had never met. He talked dates with me for a moment, and the trip was confirmed. To my astonishment, in a matter of minutes, the trip time and dates were confirmed. Tom and I were going to Houston to spend four days with people I never heard of until a few minutes earlier. But in my heart, I knew this was something that was meant to be.

I don't believe in luck or fate. I do believe in divine appointments. I sensed in my spirit that God was setting up a divine appointment. I knew that if everything I had heard that night was true, I was in for the experience of a lifetime. At that moment, I did not understand even a small portion of what was about to happen.

# FRIENDS I DIDN'T KNOW I HAD

Tom and I arrived in the Houston suburb of Spring at midnight on a Thursday night/ Friday morning. Through the assistance of GPS, we found their house and parked in front. Tom encouraged me to park in the driveway, but I thought that to be a little presumptuous. When we walked toward the front door, I was hesitant to ring their doorbell this late, but they were expecting us. After a moment, the door swung open by a tall man with auburn hair and welcoming big smile on a kind face. As we stepped inside to their formal living room, I also stepped into a friendship and journey.

Three things I would learn over the next few days. First, anyone who comes in the front door does not know them very well. Friends always come in the back door off of the driveway, and through the kitchen. Second, no one ever sits in the formal living room. Everyone who walks in the back door is a friend and sits around the kitchen and "visits." There is a small dining table, as well as a center island, where everyone sits. The dining table functions as Betty's work desk and make-up table. But there is still more than enough room for everyone to be at ease. Life is very informal at the Rex household. Thirdly, everyone parks in the driveway. They live on a small curve, and a car could easily get hit, parked in front of their house.

As I sat in the living room, I became more awestruck. It is a room unlike any I have ever seen. It appeared to me that there were several museum quality paintings positioned around the room.

More than a few of the paintings were exceptionally sizeable. You could not ignore the Madonna that hung on one wall, or the portrait of Christ. My guess was, they were somewhere near three by four feet. As I glanced through the doorway into the hall, I saw several other quality art pieces on the walls. The number of art pieces could not be ignored. Some hung on the wall and others on easels.

But the one thing that was more astonishing than anything else was Lonnie and Betty themselves. They immediately put me at ease. We sat down and they made small talk. They asked how the trip was, were we hungry or need something to drink, and how tired were we? It was as if we had come home to visit family. After a few minutes, Lonnie said our rooms were ready and waiting on us. I pulled the car into the driveway, Tom and I began unloading our luggage. I was excited about what was going to take place over the next few days, but was welcoming a little shut eye.

At that point, I learned Lonnie was different than anyone else his age or any age. He doesn't go to bed! After I unpacked, I made my way down the hall to Lonnie's office. The watch on my arm read one o'clock in the morning. I was expecting to just poke my head inside the door to say good night. When I stepped inside, Lonnie leaned back in his office chair, invited me to sit down, and the most amazing four days of my life had just started. Tom said "Lonnie why don't you tell Rick about working with Oral Roberts back in the 1950s." We were off to the races with story after story of the adventures of Lonnie Rex. In three and half days, I would record nearly fifty hours of stories on my digital recorder. A story would lead to another story. I would hear about 20th century apostles and 20th century statesmen.

Great people will teach you great truths. This is no less true with Lonnie Rex. The essence is his faith and his persistence. One truth he repeated several times over those first few days was, "I never asked God for money. I asked God for ideas. Whenever

God provided the ideas, the money would follow." This man, who was supposedly crippled by polio as a child, has raised millions of dollars for major ministries and Christian charities all over the world.

Typically he was able to do this because he brought a fresh approach to the problem. Lonnie did things differently than anyone had before. He was always looking for opportunities to learn, and do things better than he had before. God opened doors that others would have overlooked. Lonnie does not question the motives or politics of the people he works with, he just solves the problem.

This has given him an extraordinary life, which have made an impact on hundreds or thousands, if not millions around the world. Lonnie is not intimidated by anyone because he serves a God who created us all. He had worked with Catholics, Communists, and dictators. He had worked with Pentecostals, Methodists, Baptists, Muslims, Hindus, Sikhs, witch doctors, and atheists. Lonnie does not see the doctrine; he just sees the need. He solves the problems and lets God get the glory. Most people draw battle lines; Lonnie draws love lines. These are lines that lead to showing the love of Christ to people, through a hand filled with food or medicine. He allows God to judge the motives of others. Through all of the hours I have talked with him, I have never seen him speak judgment over anyone, friend, or foe. He does not betray confidences but will give advice when asked. Many ask because they know this man will share his heart and wisdom without reservation.

My goal is to share with the world some of the incredible stories that Lonnie has shared with me through the various times I have been able to visit with him. Lonnie is a man who has touched the world through his life. He is truly one of the most remarkable people that few have ever heard of.

# LIVING IN WASHINGTON, D.C.

I started one of the sessions with some questions about people Lonnie met while he lived in Washington, D.C. in the early 1950s. "Who are some of the people you met while you lived in Washington, D.C. in the early 1950s? I have heard about a story involving President Harry Truman and the car. What was that story?"

I loved President Truman. Our office was just a short distance from the White House. I would see President Truman every day when he went out on his walk. He had quite the entourage. He would stop and talk with people who were walking on the sidewalk. He was just a friendly guy from Independence, Missouri. I knew his voice well from hearing him outside on the sidewalk.

One night we were out to dinner at the Mayflower Hotel which was across the street from the White House. I told Betty, "Harry Truman is in this restaurant. I hear his voice."

About that time, Harry Truman, Bess, and Margaret his daughter, and another man, walked up to our table and said to us, "Come on outside. This is Charles Wilson, president of General Motors, and he wants to show us a prototype of a car without a post in the middle of the doors." Well we couldn't imagine such a car so we got up and walked outside. President Truman invited everyone in the restaurant to come outside and see the car. Everyone in the restaurant gets up from their table, leaving their food, and marches outside to see the car the President wants us to see. Outside was a 1951 Cadillac four door sedan without a post in the middle.

Charles Wilson got inside and rolled down all of the windows, so people could see there was no post. President Truman opened all four of the doors, so people could see how open the car was without a post. Someone in the crowd said, "What if the car rolls over?"

Charles Wilson explained they had reinforced the frame to take care of that. President Truman walked around and kicked a tire or two. People from the restaurant made over the car for a few minutes and finally everyone walked back inside the Mayflower and finished their dinner. I never saw President Truman again until the inauguration of President Eisenhower over a year later. Charles would go on to become the Secretary of Defense under Eisenhower.

Years later, Betty and I traveled with some friends on an around the world cruise on the Queen Elizabeth II. We did not do the complete cruise but we made arrangements with the Queen Elizabeth II to pick us up in Mombasa, Kenya, Africa. We traveled on the cruise for twenty-eight days. On board was the editor of the New York Times Clifton Daniel, and his wife, Margaret Truman Daniel. We were able to talk with them on the deck of the ship. She did lectures about her life in the White House. She would answer questions from the audience. I shared with her the story of seeing her father at the Mayflower with the car.

When Eisenhower was President, we took our son Royce to the annual Easter Egg roll at the White House. Royce would have been about four years old at the time. We have a picture of Royce and President Eisenhower on the White House lawn.

I got up one morning, looked at the newspaper and noticed that Winston Churchill was in town. That would have been probably 1952. I knew he would be staying at the British Embassy which was just down the street from where we lived on

Massachusetts Avenue. I got in the car and headed for the office, and as I drove past the Embassy I noticed two huge gates about a half a block apart. I noticed that on the gate on the right were all of the cameras and news people gathered to see Churchill. I thought that was odd because at the British Embassy they always drove in the left gate.

I pulled around the corner, parked and walked back to the left gate. About the time I got there I heard something from behind, turned around and there were limousines pulling in right behind me. The first car had the British Foreign Secretary, Anthony Eden in it. The second car had Churchill. I am standing right beside the gate. All of the press is half a block away. As the cars pulled in slowly I just walk beside the limousines as they pull into the embassy. As they pulled to a stop I was standing at the door of the Embassy. Churchill stepped out and assumed I was a part of the greeting party. He got out, shook my hand, did a little small talk where he spoke about the beautiful day and everything else. He continued to talk with me for few minutes. Finally Anthony Eden was walking into the embassy; he turned to Churchill and said, "Come on!" Churchill walked toward the entrance to the Embassy.

Suddenly, I find myself alone. No was there. No one questioned my right to be there. I started back down the driveway. As you know I have a quite a limp. As a started down the driveway, the press started walking up the drive. They had finally figured out Churchill had come up the left gate. As I walked through the crowd of press, they parted for me to walk through. When I was almost to my car I heard footsteps behind me. One of the press shouted out at me, "The limp doesn't throw us! We know you are with Scotland Yard!" I never looked back, just got in my car and drove to work.

A great person in the church world at that time was the pastor of the New York Avenue Presbyterian Church, Peter Marshall. He later became the chaplain of the United States Senate. We didn't attend the church, but from time to time we would stop by the church. Peter Marshall was a very gracious man. He would come out of his office and talk with us a few minutes. He was from Scotland and spoke with the strong Scottish brogue. You would never know how important and influential he was by talking with him. We only heard him preached once. I heard him pray several times when he would open the Senate.

Betty and I walked past the New York Avenue Presbyterian Church on Sundays when we were going to the church we attended. Many of the streets in Washington are on a triangle. New York Avenue is one of those. It was on an angle because of this. But there were sidewalks all around the church. On Sundays there would be a crowd for two blocks waiting to get inside for the next service. He was very popular.

A couple of times a year we would take the train up to New York City and attend the Marble Collegiate Church and listen to Dr. Norman Vincent Peale speak. We would take the train up on Saturday night, spend the night and go to church the next morning. We always loved to eat at Momma Leoni's Italian restaurant. Betty and I loved to hear him preach. The first Sunday we went there the place was packed. In fact, we would go to the eleven o'clock service. The crowd would be lined up around the block waiting for the earlier service to dismiss so they could get inside. They would walk out one door and the next crowd would walk into a different door.

I was so excited to hear him the first time we went. He came out and looked around and there was a little stand right beside his chair. Dr. Peale closed his eyes all of the time the choir sang. I thought he was sound asleep! Every once in a while when something happened he would open one eye and look at the program and go back to sleep. When I saw him do this I thought to myself, *Wow, this is strange!* Finally when it came his turn, someone said, "Here is Dr. Peale," he continued to sit in his chair. Dr. Peale waited until the place got totally silent, he jumped up from the chair and stepped into the pulpit with gusto and didn't stop for the next 45 minutes.

Years later, we were back in Washington for another function. This was in the late seventies when Jimmy Carter was the President. Betty and I decided to attend the Baptist church where the Carters attended. It was well known that Carter was Southern Baptist and he taught a Bible class at the church. We walked into the church early so we could get a good seat. Sunday School was still in session. We got down to the second or third row. President Carter was teaching his class in the balcony.

When Sunday School was over, the auditorium started filling up until it was packed. We were excited to be in the service. The lady in front of us began to chat with us. She asked us where we were from and why were we in Washington? She told us that her husband was a Deacon at the church. She said he had been a Deacon at the church for several years. The service started with hymns as churches do. All of the sudden, someone jumps up and starts to shout, protesting something the President was doing. The protester was just a few rows behind us. The church ushers quickly reached the man, one grabbed him by the shoulders and the other grabbed his feet and away they took him up the aisle and out of the auditorium as he screamed at the top of his lungs every step of the way.

Everything started back like nothing had happened. A few minutes later another protester stood and began to shout. This time it was a woman. The ushers grabbed her like she was a small child. An usher threw her over his shoulder and carried her out as she continued to shout. When this happened, the deacon's wife in front of us turned around, and I have to quote her exact words, "This makes me so mad! We had a good church before that D—n Carter came in!"

I lived in Washington, DC, for four years. During that time, I learned three things. I learned how to make money, how to spend money and how to save money. In 1955 when I moved to Tulsa, one of the people I met there was a realtor. This was when they first instituted Urban Renewal. Urban Renewal had mapped out downtown Tulsa to decide what they were going to tear down. On the edge of that area was a five story building owned by Bethlehem Steel. Two years before Bethlehem Steel had spent a million dollars rehabbing the building. This was in 1955 when a million dollars was a lot of money. It had marble halls and stairs. It had plush carpet everywhere else. It had an appraisal of two and a half million dollars. The appraisal was about two inches thick.

I was talking with the realtor one day and he threw the appraisal at me, he said, "Do you want this thing? I'm not going to fool with it. You can't do anything with Urban Renewal. No one wants to buy it because nobody knows what is going to happen." I said, "sure, I'll take it." I took the appraisal home.

Now this is what Washington, DC, taught me. Brash, go to the top and never say I can't do it. I called Bethlehem Steel in Bethlehem, Pennsylvania. I reached the secretary and treasurer of Bethlehem Steel Company. They had moved their Tulsa office to Lubbock, Texas, and the building in Tulsa was sitting empty. It was caught up in Urban Renewal and no one wanted it. I said to the company executive, "Sir, do you still have that building in Tulsa, Oklahoma?"

"Yeah. What will you give me for it?"

Without hesitation I said to him, "I will give you $90,000." At that point, I expected him to throw down the telephone, but I was surprised.

"Mr. Rex. We are having a board meeting this afternoon. Would you please call me back at five o'clock and I will give you an answer." It was about five o'clock when I called him.

I don't know where the figure of $90,000 came from. I probably had about two hundred dollars in the bank. But at five o'clock I called him back. When he got on the phone he said, "Mr. Rex this is November 2. Can you close by November 30?"

I replied, "Yes sir."

He said, "If you can close by November 30, we will accept your offer of $90,000. November 30 is the end of our fiscal year and this will get this property off our books."

I still had no idea where I would get the money. That night the Lord gave me an idea. I never ask the Lord for money. I ask him for ideas. The next morning, I told Betty to get dressed; we were driving to Dallas that day. I had a ten thousand dollar life insurance policy with Republic National Life in Dallas. At that time, that was a lot of money. We drove to Dallas to their headquarters. I walked my way all the way up to a vice-president of the company. I had the appraisal with me. When I got the vice-president he said, "How can I help you?"

I told him, "I want a loan on this building. Here is the appraisal."

He looked at the bottom line of the appraisal and said to me, "How much money do you want?"

Without hesitancy I said, "A million dollars." I knew I would need the extra money to make payments until I could figure out what to do with the building.

The executive replied, "Mr. Rex, you take your wife shopping at Neiman-Marcus. We are having a board meeting this afternoon of Republic National Life. Come back at five o'clock and I will give you the answer."

I took Betty shopping at Neiman-Marcus and was back at Republic National Life about five o'clock. When we got back there they led us into a small room where there was barely enough room for three people. The executive said, "Mr. Rex, we are not going to loan you a million dollars on this building."

In the back of my mind I was thinking, *Well, I will take a half a million if I have to.*

The vice-president continued, "We are going to loan you, $1,050,000. Your note will be for $1,100,000. You are paying $50,000 down today on a motel we took back at courthouse steps last Friday. We don't want to run it. We will close on the motel today."

I had no idea where the motel was in Tulsa. I had never run a motel in my life. It was on Highway 66, near 11th Street. It was a style that was popular in the 1950s. It was individual cabins with an attached single car garage. There were thirty units in all.

I said, "Okay!"

I left his office with a check for a million dollars. Two days later, I went to the attorney's office for Bethlehem Steel and paid them for the office building. We owned the motel for eleven years. Sometime later, I leased the office building for a tech school. This is why I say I learned three things in Washington: how to make money, how to spend money, and how to bless others.

Those principles have served me well during my life. I was able to invest in real estate and other investments, so I could provide a good life for my family. Those lessons have served me well throughout my life. There is no reason for Christian people to be poor. Many times because of these investments, I was able to bless many people through my charity.

# WORKING WITH ORAL ROBERTS

"**L**onnie, tell me about working with Oral Roberts. Didn't you start back in the 1950s?"

While we were living in Washington, D.C. Oral came to town for a meeting. They had the services in an armory. He was very infatuated with Demos Shakarian and the Full Gospel Businessmen Association. He said, "Lonnie, let's organize the second chapter of the Full Gospel Businessmen. So I got a group of guys together and picked up Oral one Saturday morning, went to breakfast with everyone and we organized the second chapter of the Full Gospel Businessmen. The first was in Los Angeles. We organized the second in D.C. The man Francis Robinson, whom we appointed president, retained that leadership for life.

While I worked with Oral with this, it gave us the chance to renew our friendship. I had known Oral for a long time, ever since he succeeded my dad as the pastor of the First Pentecostal Holiness Church in Enid. Oral was a just a young guy then. It was a few years before he went into full time evangelism. I asked Oral how things were going with his ministry.

Oral said, "Lonnie, I just started filming the Crusades and going on television. But no television stations want to broadcast a healing evangelist. Right now I am just on four UHF stations."

This was long before cable. I remember one station was in Decatur, Alabama. I don't think the signal went to the edge of town. After Oral left Washington I got a call from his office asking me to come to work with Oral Roberts and sell his program to the television stations. This was 1955. I had a great job making about a thousand a week. Oral offered me a thousand a month, which wasn't bad for the time. But Betty and I wanted to go back to Oklahoma. We wanted our children to be closer to family. But I really felt an ordination in my life to do this.

While working with Oral in Washington with Full Gospel Businessmen, I learned something about Oral I had not known before. When Oral got nervous he had to go to the bathroom. When I picked him up that Saturday to go to the breakfast, before we got there he said to me, "Lonnie, find a station. I have to go to the bathroom."

I didn't think much of it; I found a station. He got out of the car and went inside, came back and we finished our trip. When we got to the place for the breakfast meeting, before he got out of the car, Oral said to me, "Lonnie, do you know where the men's room is, I need to go again."

Well, this was twice in less than a half hour. I thought he might be sick. I asked him if he was okay. He said, "No, I am nervous."

I was shocked. I said, "Oral, how can you be nervous? You spoke to ten thousand people last night. There won't be more than a few dozen men at the meeting this morning."

Oral told me, "I can speak to ten thousand people, look over their head and it doesn't bother me a bit. But when I have to look twenty people in the eye when I talk to them, I get nervous." Even great men have issues sometimes in their lives.

One of things I did while I worked for Oral was help him answer the letters his supporters sent him. One of things that set Oral apart in the early days was that he answered his mail. There were other radio preachers but when people wrote them they got no response. Oral had his first big meeting in 1948. He had the Living Waters trio of Laverne Dryden and his wife Bonnie and her sister, Aunt Lovie Miller. Oral developed a radio ministry which was broadcast on several stations around the country. Oral had developed paragraphs that could be used to answer the letters people mailed to the ministry. When I got there in 1955, I started rewriting the paragraphs every month.

The first day I went to work for Oral Roberts, he called me into his office and said, "Lonnie, I am embarrassed. I cannot get on television in my hometown. We have tried and tried."

At that time Oral was on only four television stations across the country. All of the stations were UHF stations. They were all very weak. He went on to say, "I am very embarrassed that we can't get on here."

I was in my twenties. I was very brash, I knew it all. Nothing could stop me. I had learned about all of this stuff in Washington. I said to Oral, "That's all right; I will take care of that *today*. What else do you want me to do?"

Oral said, "Just get me on in Tulsa."

I left the office, got me a television reel of his broadcast and proceeded to go the local stations. I went to Channel 2, the NBC affiliate, and they threw me out. I went to channel 6, the CBS affiliate, they cussed me out. I went to channel 8, the ABC channel, and they refused to let me in the door. They didn't want anything to do with Oral Roberts. I was told to not come back. Now I was embarrassed because of my brash statements, so I couldn't go back to the office. I considered making my first day my last day. "If I can't do this, why am I here?"

Betty was placing pressure on me to move to Oklahoma City. We had been away for four years in Washington. She missed being close to her family and church friends. I was questioning why I had moved to Tulsa and gone to work for Oral anyway. But I read in the paper that they were having a Rolls Royce car club meeting at the Trade Winds Motel there in Tulsa. I decided to go because I had always been intrigued by the Rolls Royce. I went down there. People were everywhere. They were giving ribbons to some of the cars. After a while most of the people were leaving.

This man walked up to me and said, "You must be new around here. What's your name and what do you do?"

I said, "I'm Lonnie Rex and I work with the Oral Roberts television department."

He then ducked his head. He didn't extend his hand to shake hands or anything. He just stood there. After a moment, I began to be embarrassed. Finally, I said, "Who are you and what do you do?"

Finally, he said, "My name is Jimmy Leake and I own channel 8 television. How can I help you?"

I said, "I want to put Oral Roberts on your television station."

Jimmy ducked his head again. Looking up he, said, "What day?" He ducked his head again.

I said, "Sunday morning."

Jimmy said, "What time?" Then he ducked his head again.

I said, "Eight o'clock."

Jimmy looked me square in the eye and said, *"You got it."*

That was my first real meaningful experience with how God opens the door. Leads you and guides you. I have found that most Christians believe that when they accept Christ He lives within them. But they only believe that on Sunday mornings between ten and twelve, Sunday night between six and eight and Wednesday night between seven and eight. This was my first shock that Christ lives with you every day. He will always lead and guide you. I told everyone at the office that we were going to be on television on Channel 8 at eight o'clock Sunday morning. No one believed me. I told them to just tune in and see. Oral Roberts was on Channel 8 at eight o'clock every Sunday morning for over twenty-five years.

I have always prayed for ideas. When God gives you an idea it is his responsibility to follow through and open the doors and make it possible. I got an idea. I spoke to Oral Roberts and said, "Oral will you let me write every television station in America and offer them our television program?"

Oral replied, "We can't do that! We don't have that much money. You've gone crazy!"

I said, "No, just listen to me. I am going to offer them because we have a jewel of a program. I am going to offer to LET them run our program for free for the first ninety days. After that we will pay them twenty-five percent of the normal price for religious programming. The next ninety days we will pay fifty per cent of their religious price. The next ninety days we will pay seventy-five percent of their religious price. At the end of the year we will be paying the full rate for religious programming."

Finally and very reluctantly, Oral agreed to the plan. He left Tulsa and went on a crusade out of town. I composed a letter and sent it to every television station in America. In sixty days we went from six stations, including channel 8, to where we covered 94% of all of the homes within the forty-eight states. That was a really great answer to prayer. That was the beginning of what the Oral Roberts Evangelistic Association would become.

Then I got brave and ask if I could write the radio stations. Well, because that had become so successful, he agreed. At that time, they had been broadcasting a radio program for about eight years. They were up to about 125 radio stations nationwide. Within sixty days of writing the letter to the radio stations, we were on over five hundred radio stations across the country. I was the guy who handled all of the arrangements with all of the stations. I worked on the contracts and agreements with the stations. This was a long time before faxes or email. We had to do all of this by telephone and the United States Post Office. But all of this happened within a couple of months.

For that first year, I thought this was the reason God had sent me to work with Oral Roberts. Oral filmed the healing lines in the tent meetings. This was considered very radical for the time. It became my job to go to Chicago. They might film a thousand people in the healing line over a period of ten days. It was my job to select five that could go in a television program. If you want to be in the healing line, you signed a card, which included a release to be on the television program. It also included their name, address and telephone number. That's how we got our mailing list to contact them through our magazine and appeal letters.

I would choose the ones I thought were the best for television. I wanted people who were emotional. I wanted people who seemed to believe in what God was doing. Then, I would take the cards back to Tulsa, and contact the people. I wanted to make sure they were still alive. I wanted to make sure they were still walking in their healing and let them know they were going to be on television. This work really consumed all of my time.

This generated a lot of mail. Oral had devised a letter opening system. If they got a thousand letters in today, he had readers that would read the mail. Oral had about two hundred paragraphs that each reader had. When the reader would read it, she would say that paragraphs 38, 42 and 83 address these issues. The writer is asking for prayer for a brother, sister or mother or someone. They had a paragraph that was supposed to answer every letter. If there was no answer that fit they would send the letter to a specialist that would answer the letter. At times it was my responsibility to write those paragraphs. I took this very heavy hearted because I knew what the letters meant to these people.

About a month after I started doing this I found out what this meant. We attended a Pentecostal Holiness Camp Meeting in Ada, Oklahoma. They would have hundreds of people bring their tents for ten days and attend services five times a day. We drove up in front of Betty's grandmother's tent. Before we could get out of the car, grandma ran out to the car and came up to my window. She reached inside her bra to the point it was almost embarrassing. She pulled out a wad of paper. She began to unfold it and while she was doing that she said at the top of her voice, "I got a special letter from Oral!"

She handed me the letter. I knew I had written all of the paragraphs in that letter. I wanted to say, "Grandma, I wrote all of those letters."

She went on to say, "Oral signed it himself!"

I knew the letter had been signed by a machine. But I saw the excitement and anticipation in her voice. Oral would tell people to put the letter where they had problems or were hurting. That was why grandma had placed the letter in her bra. Unknown to us she had breast cancer. When I gave the letter back to her, she refolded it and placed it back in her bra where she needed the prayer answered. I saw the hope in her eyes that letter gave to her. That gave me the foundation, for all of my letter writing success.

This was when the ministry really took off. We went from a few hundred letters every day to thousands of letters each day. We got more mail than anyone else in Tulsa. The only address we announced on television or radio was; Oral Roberts, Tulsa, Oklahoma. We didn't use an address and this was before zip codes. During this time Oral was forced to build a seven story Marble building, an unusual building with no windows. It provided the space for the ministry.

A large ministry will attract all sorts of people. We had three people who would attend the crusades to go out in the crowds to obtain subscriptions to the ministry magazine, Healing Waters. The arrangement was that half of the money would go to the salesperson and half would go to the ministry. There was one lady who was a star salesman. She came to us from working at Streets department store in Tulsa. She was an attractive lady who had no problems convincing people to subscribe to the magazine.

I came home between Crusades, went to the office and spoke with G.H. Montgomery. I had known him since I was a kid. He had dedicated my father's new church building at Enid, Oklahoma. G.H. said, "Lonnie, I need your help. You know Ms. So-and-so? I had to fire her today."

I said, "What do you mean? She is our best salesman. Everybody loves her."

Montgomery said, "I had to fire her. She has been going around telling people at the crusades that she is pregnant with

Oral's baby. I called her in today. I asked her if she was telling everybody that she was pregnant with Oral's baby. She admitted she was. Would you please tell me, when and where was the baby conceived?"

She told him, "It's immaculate conception."

The following Sunday morning, she was at Evangelistic Temple and Oral happened to be home, she was sitting behind Oral and Evelyn. By this time Oral and Evelyn knew the story. They were very upset that she was sitting behind them. She had just been fired. They complained to Pastor West. They explained the situation to him.

The following Wednesday night, I went to church. Pastor West had called her in and forbid her to come to church. He came out of his office and said to me, "Lonnie, I know you know all about this. I've told her she can't come back to church."

I said, "Brother West, she will be here Sunday morning. The woman has no rationalization."

He said, "Oh no, bless God, she won't be here. I made it very clear."

The following Sunday morning there was Oral and Evelyn and the whole family with this lady sitting right behind them. It created quite a stir. She not only attended services but she wrote a letter to every Assembly of God pastor telling them that story. Several of us had to get on the phone and call every Assembly of God pastor and tell them the truth. The lady was not mentally there."

Oral called me in again and said, "I want to be on the Mutual Radio Network."

This was probably the largest radio network in the country at that time. They had some religious programming but not a lot. I contacted the Mutual Network. We worked out the time and the price. But because of internal politics, Oral didn't get the word in time, there was no decision made, and we didn't get on Mutual. Oral was not happy but now he decided he wanted to be on ABC in New York City. I said okay. I got ABC in New York City. It was a good time slot but it was expensive. I told my bosses. One of them said to me, "Oral doesn't need this. It is too expensive. I am not going to bother him with this." When Oral got back I told Oral directly what his options were.

This upset the people above me. While Oral was gone on a crusade, they fired me the week before Christmas. This upset me and it upset Betty. We thought we were in the will of God. I asked to meet with Oral and Evelyn directly. We were still going to the same church together. On Sunday afternoon, Betty and I met with Oral and Evelyn in his office. Everyone knew what had happened. The older guys in the office got tired of the new guy showing them up, so they fired me. After we talked, Oral said he had to stand behind the men at the office. Then Evelyn said to me, "Lonnie, someday you will look back at this and see this was one of the best decisions that ever happened to you in your life."

I thought that was the stupidest thing anyone had ever said. In those days when someone went to work for the ministry, they could borrow the down payment money for a house from the ministry. I had borrowed three thousand dollars for a down payment. I had bought a brand new three bedroom, two bath, two car garage house for $13,500. I signed a note for the down payment money. About two weeks after that, I got the note in the mail cancelled.

Evelyn Roberts was an important part of the ministry, but she was more behind the scenes. But she was an active part of the radio ministry. She would read the letters people had written on the air. Every Sunday morning we would meet down at the radio studio between 7:30 and 8:00 and record the broadcast. We did this before we went to church. We all went to the same church at the time, Evangelistic Temple.

Oral and Evelyn lived out in the country near Bixby. One Sunday morning during service, Evelyn walked down to the front and whispered in the ear of the pastor that she needed a time of prayer. The pastor announced to the congregation, "Evelyn Roberts feels the need for prayer this morning and anyone who would like to join her should come on down and pray."

Several people came down for prayer. They anointed Evelyn with oil and prayed for her. I was playing the organ and Betty was playing the piano while people were praying. When the pastor started praying for others, Evelyn came over and sat on the organ bench beside me. She was weeping, almost the level of sobbing. Finally through her tears she said, "I am just so mad at that Oral Roberts! My back has been hurting all week. Oral had to get up early this morning and go speak at a men's breakfast. He was up and dressed, and I was still in my robe. When he walked out the front door, I ran after him. I told him that my back had been hurting all week and I needed him to pray for me."

He turned to me in the middle of the driveway and said, "I will be on the radio in twenty minutes. Go to the radio and lay your hands on the radio.

It was the hardest thing in the world for me not to laugh. But she continued, "Now I know how those old ladies feel."

Photo 4 (Richard Roberts)

I knew all of the Roberts family including Evelyn's parents, her sister and step brother. At one time or another, I had all four of the Roberts' kids in my choir at Evangelistic Temple. I was instrumental in creating the romance between Oral's daughter Rebecca and Marshall Nash. He had come to Tulsa in the summer of 1957 to visit his brother. Oral was going to have a meeting in Tyler, Texas. Marshall wanted to go to the meeting. He talked to me and said, "Lonnie if you will loan me $300, I want to go and I will set up a pop stand. People would come early to the afternoon meetings to get a good seat. I will sell them pop.

I loaned him the money. He went to Tyler for the entire ten days. When he got back he repaid the money. He did quite well at the meeting. While he was there, he met Rebecca Roberts. They started dating and eventually got married. The silly kids were very happy until 1977 when they took off in a plane from Denver in a snow storm. They crashed into the side of a mountain.

Betty and I had a strong relationship with Oral and Evelyn after I left their employ. One day, Oral called me on the phone and said, "Lonnie, I know you will tell me the truth. Why don't my donors come to the City of Faith?"

The City of Faith hospital had been completed for a couple of years. Oral was just sure his donors would travel to Tulsa to go to the City of Faith. He was shocked that it wasn't full. So I said to him, "Oral, I will tell you my opinion. You know, there is no one who adores you like my dad and my mother."

He said, "Yes, I know that."

I said, "They only live in Oklahoma City, which is only a hundred miles away. But when they get sick or have a heart attack or something. They run to their local hospital. They would never think of driving a hundred miles to Tulsa. When my mother had to do a selective surgery on her nose for cancer, we brought her over here and she was in your hospital and they did a great job. But on anything that it is emergency or is not elective, I don't care how much your donors love you, they are not going to come here."

I went on, "I also must tell you this. I was out at your hospital a few weeks ago. I was getting ready to go to Africa and I mentioned that to one of your doctor friends we both know. He said, come out to the hospital and let us do a complete check-up on you before you go to Africa. I thought that was a good idea so I came out to the City of Faith one morning about eight o'clock and checked in. They did this test and that test, and worked me over. When I left the hospital that evening, they said I needed to write out a check for $902." I told Oral that I could check in to any hospital in town and have a heart operation and get released and won't have to pay a dime because I have Blue Cross and Blue Shield. The City of Faith said that I should turn in the bill to my insurance company and they would reimburse me. I sent in the bill for $902 and after about thirty days got a check for $312. They said this test City of Faith charges $100 and we pay $15.

Oral said, "Do you have a copy of that bill?"

I said, "I have it right here."

He said, "Fax that to Ruth Brooks (his secretary).

Oral was stunned. The next day Ruth Brooks called me. "Lonnie, I have given direct orders to the hospital that your dad, your mother, and you are on a special list. You come to the hospital, and you will only be charged what the insurance pays." We took advantage of that several times because of emergency situations.

One of the moments I really cherish in my relationship with Oral and Evelyn happened in Dallas. Betty and I had been down to Mexico for some project there. Coming back we had to change planes in Dallas. As we are sitting in the airport, I look up and all of the sudden here comes Oral and Evelyn. I jump up and go over into the middle of the aisle. When they see me they stop. Evelyn had a big bag on her arm and Oral had a suit bag he was carrying. I held up my arms and they come to meet me. Oral throws his suit bag on the floor. Grabbed me and hugged me around the neck. He laid his head on my shoulder. He spoke into my ear and said, "Lonnie I have loved you for so many years."

Oral was not a hugger. He was not a toucher. That so shocked me. I backed off, Oral said, "I preached for Brother Creflo Dollar this morning and we are on our way home."

They went over and spoke to Betty as well. We were on standby but were able to go home with them on the same plane.

Another time, I got a call about two o'clock in the afternoon. I was told they were having a special partners meeting that night and Oral and Evelyn have asked that you and Betty be at the side door at a quarter of seven. That was all I knew. I told Betty we were going to go. We were met at the door; we were taken in, and sat on the front row. A few moments after we were seated, Oral came out to begin the service with Evelyn walking behind him. Richard and Lindsay walked in behind Evelyn. They had just got married. I had never seen Lindsay before. After them was their daughter Roberta Potts and her husband. I thought she might have been the one to make sure we were invited. She loved us. She went to school with our son Royce and she would come to our house when she was young.

Just as the service was concluding, an usher walked over to me and whispered in my ear, "Oral wants to see you behind stage."

So we walked behind the stage. Oral came into the room and greeted us. Evelyn came in as well. Again he gave me a big hug. It really shocked me again. Evelyn grabbed me up to my elbows and started crying. She said, "Lonnie you know, I have lost two children."

She knew I have been very close to all of her children including the two she had lost. I said to her, "Evelyn, you have two left. Hang on to them for all you got."

With that she turned and left. In a few moments, Richard and Lindsay came through and left. Then Roberta and her husband came through and left. All of the sudden, Betty and I are standing behind stage all alone. I was really stunned by everything. I wasn't sure why they had called and why they wanted us there. I looked around the curtain and saw Dr. Carl Hamilton, long time provost of ORU. I taught Carl in high school. I grabbed him and said, "Carl, what's this all about?"

He said, "Lonnie, I have seen this several times lately. It's as if an old man is getting ready to die, and he is trying to make it right with everybody." With those words, he turned around and walked away. I don't know everything that day meant but the experience has stayed with me.

Years later, after Evelyn and Oral had died. I crossed paths with the travel agent who I knew made all of Richard Roberts' travel arrangements. I said to him, "Rick, do you ever see Richard?" This was about six months after the trouble at ORU had started.

He said, "No, but I talk with him everyone once in a while. I still make all of his travel arrangements."

I told him, "If you ever talk to Richard, tell him hello from ole' Lonnie."

Two hours later I had a call. "Can you meet with Richard Roberts in his office tomorrow at 4:30?"

I thought to myself, *my Lord what am I going to say?* I took him one of my dad's books. It has pictures of the Enid church in it. I told him this was his heritage because he was born in Enid. Then I said to him, "Richard, I don't know why I said I wanted to come over and talk with you. I don't have any questions. Everything I know is what I read in the papers. I don't have anything to condemn. All I wanted to come over and say is, we love Richard. Betty and I love Richard. We've known you since you were a little kid and we still love Richard."

Then I said, "I wasn't going to tell you this. As bad as this thing is. As much as some people had betrayed you. One day you are going to say this was the best thing that ever happened to you." I was quoting his mother.

With that he broke down. I went on to say, "Richard, you have a fifteen year history with television. You are the face of Oral Roberts Evangelistic Association. Those people didn't give to ORU. They were giving to Richard. You told them where to put it. Now the ministry is going to receive more money than it has ever received. You won't have to share that money." It was like it was the first time he had thought of that. He brightened up and hugged me and hugged me.

Later he has told me several times he is glad to have me back in his life. For years we would run into him in the neighborhood. When we would vote and out shopping. But now the relationship has been renewed. I told him that since he had started a humanitarian work in his crusades, if I could help him, I was there for him. Within a month, we had two and a half million dollars' worth of children's vitamins we were able to distribute.

We all have gifts that God has given us. You have yours, others have theirs, and I have mine. God has gifted me to raise funds for ministries. The ideas God gave me for the Oral Roberts Evangelistic Association helped set the groundwork for what has become Oral Roberts Ministries. I give God the glory but he gave me the ideas to help all of the ministries I have worked for over the years.

# TL OSBORN EVANGELISTIC ASSOCIATION

We salute the valuable humanitarian work you and your foundation are accomplishing for the remarkable peoples of Russia and so many other nations.

—T.L. Osborn

I knew TL and Daisy because their kids sang in my choir at Evangelistic Temple. Betty played the piano and I directed the choir. I wasn't working for Oral, but I was helping Billy James Hargis. TL knew I had helped Oral with some of the films. TL called me about four o'clock on a Friday afternoon. I was sick with the flu and didn't give a hoot about talking with anybody. TL said, "Lonnie, I am in a real fix. I just got back from Africa and I have raw footage of a film and we need somebody to put music and sound effects with it. How long would it take you to do that?"

I said, "How long is the film?"

He said, "It is about an hour to an hour and ten minutes."

I told him, "With that long a film, I would probably need four, five and maybe even six weeks. That would score it, get the players, record it, sound effects, all this. When do you need it?"

He replied, "First thing Monday morning."

"This coming Monday morning," I came back with a little surprise in my voice. "Well the only way I can do it is for you to bring a projector to Evangelistic Temple first thing in the morning. Bring a projectionist. He needs to be prepared to run it all day. I will score the music and the sound effects it needs.

Tomorrow night, you and Daisy can come down to the church and read the narration with the music background."

Lonnie playing music for a TL movie

They brought a projector and their son to the church the next morning to run it. I worked all day writing the music the best that I could. That night Daisy and TL came to the church, and recorded the narration. I hooked them up to a microphone, TL would talk and then Daisy. While they did this, I played the music. They loved it. I said to them, "In order to have this for Monday morning you need to meet me at the Oral Roberts recording studio tomorrow night after church. We will finish recording everything there."

So the next night after church, they met me there. I had made all of the arrangements. I had my music and my sound effects. I set up the microphones. We did the entire film in one take. That one take has been on that film for over fifty years.

Later that week, TL asked me if I could join his team as his Business Manager. I told him that I would have to give two weeks' notice where I was. TL was okay with that, so I agreed to go to work for him. I went to work for him on October 15, 1957.

The first day I went to work for TL Osborn, he was out of the country in crusades. The girls in the office showed me the letters the ministry had received that day. Some CPA had given them such a complicated routine to safe guard them with the money that it was crazy. Every letter that came in had to have eleven check marks before it went out. They had to write down the name of everyone who sent a letter. Then they had to check that the letter was opened. Then they had to check that the letter was read. Then they had to check if the letter was opened. Then they checked if the letter had been typed. Then they had to check the letter had been placed in an envelope. Check that the letter had been mailed.

Lonnie at work with TL Osborn

This was taking so much time that it was difficult to get the mailed opened and answered. One of the girls said they were behind and there was some mail in the vault. I asked for the vault combination and TL's sister Iletta, brought me the combination. We opened the vault. There was mail stacked nearly four feet high that had never been opened. I took it all out. I opened every letter. Deposited $90,000 that day! I threw the old ledger away. Every day we would open all of the mail and answer all of the mail. TL and Daisy were shocked when I sent them the deposit slip.

When I went to work with TL, one of the first things I did was help him start a radio ministry. I knew all the stations because I had worked with them while I was with Oral. I thought it was a natural for him. We also made more films. We had eight or ten film "ministers" who took those films and would book them in churches across America, across England, and across Germany. They would show the films, take an offering, and get their names. That is how we built the tremendous mailing list that we had for TL Osborn.

Photo T.L Osborn

One of the things I did while I was with TL Osborn was organize twenty-five crusades in Germany, Switzerland, Austria, and Great Britain. In each country, we would take up the names of the people who attended. I would register the ministry in those countries and open offices. It was those countries where we would raise the most money for the ministry because no one else was asking for money from them.

We had offices in Australia, New Zealand, and Canada as well. We were the only group trying to raise money in those countries. Some people say I was the guru of direct mail for Christian organizations and ministries.

One of the first crusades I went on with TL was in Northern India, Lucknow. I went ahead of TL and set up everything for the crusade. We had to build the platform out of bricks. Lumber was very expensive but brick was cheaper. We had poles set up with lighting and speakers. I set up the chairs, the PA system and got ready for the first night. We all stayed in a little hotel near there. During the service, the word came that the local Hindu leader declared our service was not welcome. Local Hindu thugs started in the back of the crowd, clubbing people and disrupting the service as they walked forward. The local pastors shouted to us to run for our lives. We ran to the hotel to grab our stuff. The local Christian pastors surrounded the place to keep us safe. They stayed with us until we were in our cars, driving away from the place. We drove down to South India where were to have our next crusade.

Osborn still had a burden for India. When we left the crowd in North India, I went to Madras, to set up a crusade. That didn't pan out, so I went further south to Madurai. It is the second largest city in India. It dates back two millennia. It is one of the oldest continuously inhabited cities in the world. It has been inhabited since 350 B.C. That is where I set up the great Madurai crusade, and we filmed the Athens of India story. India has been a great part of my life. TL Osborn returned to Madurai in 2011 for a reunion crusade, where thousands of ministers and churches gathered to celebrate the 1958 Crusade.

We were in India getting ready to organize another Crusade. We were in New Delhi. The missionaries had loaned us a 1934 Chevrolet to drive. This was in 1958. But the steering was so bad you had to constantly steer it dramatically to the left and then to the right to keep it in the middle of the road. I was trying to drive it, TL was in the passenger seat. I nearly scared him to death! He told me, "Lonnie, give this back to the missionaries because you are going to kill somebody. If you hit somebody here they will throw us out of the car and maul us!" I gave the car back to the missionaries.

The missionaries told me the new Hindustani car was the only one sold in India. They were the only one made in India. They cost about $3,000 new. TL told me to take $3,000 and go buy a new Hindustani so we would be safe. He knew we would be coming back for more crusades and the car would be used in the future. In the meantime the missionaries could use it.

I hired a human rickshaw and had him take me down to the Hindustani dealer. I walk into the dealer. They have several models on the showroom floor. I pick out a blue one. I walk up to a salesman and told him I want the blue car. He tells me to fill out some paperwork, give him a deposit, and I should get my car within seven years. There was a waiting list of seven years for a new Hindustani car.

I told him I had to have one today! He told me that I would not get a car today but if I place a $200 deposit, if someone cancels their order I might get one in two or three years. I was really upset. I felt defeated. TL had told me to get a car and we needed a car!

I knew the people of India hated the English. They had been an English colony and just received their Independence about a decade earlier. Before I left for India the Holy Spirit prompted me to buy a great big ten gallon hat at Tenners. I didn't want anyone to confuse me for an Englishman. They would stone Englishmen! The people had seen enough American cowboy and Indian movies that they knew what the hat meant. I wore that hat everywhere I went while I was there.

I got in my rickshaw. I told the driver to take me to the Ministry of Transportation. He trots down the street, little him pulling big me. He drops me off in front of this huge building. I walk up to the door in my big hat, the door opens, I ask people where to go. One will point one way and I walk that way. Then I got somewhere else, asked directions and walked the way they told me to walk. If they said climb the stairs, I climbed the stairs. I finally got to a door that said, Minister of Transportation.

They opened the door and I walked in. There was a little guy sitting behind the longest desk I had ever seen in my life. It seemed like it was twenty feet long. He was sitting cross-legged in an Indian chair. I walked up to him. His eyes were big as saucers. He said to me, "What do you want"?

I just sit down in a chair, right in front of him. I said, "My name is Lonnie Rex. I am from Tulsa, Oklahoma. I have a film crew with me. We want to film your great country. We want to go all over your great country and film some of your great places. We want to show your beautiful country to the American people."

He said, "Oh. How can I help you?"

I said, "I want a new Hindustani car."

He said, "What color?"

"Blue", I said.

He paused for a moment and said, "Can we have tea?"

I said, "Yes."

Tea in a former English colony is always a ritual. In a few moments they bring in the tea set and we begin the ritual of having tea." He leans across to me and says, "Can you come to my house for dinner"?

I told him, "Sure, but can I bring my film crew with me?"

He agreed for me to bring the film crew. We sat and talked back and forth for a few minutes. Different staff members were coming in and out while we talked. He would speak to them in their native language. In a few minutes he leaned over and handed me a set of keys. He said, "Here are the keys to your car. It is sitting outside. You know they cost $3,000."

I said, "Yes sir, I brought a check." I wrote out the check. I walked out of the Ministry of Transportation and got in the new car. God gave me the victory!

India was a special place for TL He held several crusades there, mainly in South India. John Osteen also a heart for India. He and TL were very close. The last time I saw John Osteen, I was coming home from India and had stopped at a hotel in Bombay. I didn't know that John was staying there too. But we had a chance to visit with each other.

I came out of my room and heard a very distinctive voice. I looked down the hall and a man was leaning over saying, "I can't get this key in this door."

Recognizing the distinctive voice of John Osteen I walked down and while he was leaning over I slapped him on the back and said, "John!"

He jumped up and said, "Oh, I thought the Lord was calling me!" We were so shocked to see each other.

I said, "John, go in and call Dodie now! I have just talked to Betty and she said something big has happened to Jimmy Swaggart. It is all over the television news but she doesn't know the whole story." Dodie gave him the scandalous story of Jimmy Swaggart.

We got a much better reception in Austria than Lucknow. We had permission to do a ten day crusade in the park in Salzburg, Austria. It began to build because pastors from Germany, Switzerland, Holland, and all over that part of Europe began to come. By the time three or four days passed, we knew it was going to swell. One night TL was on the platform and announced to the pastors, "You see that big old boy over there pointing at me? Give him your name, address, and telephone number. God is putting it on my heart that I may come back to Europe this fall. If you want me to come to your city, give him your name and address."

By the time the crusade was over I had about forty names and addresses of pastors who wanted the TL Osborn Evangelistic Association to come to their town. The rest of the crusade team packed up and went back to Tulsa. They left this old boy in Europe by himself. I had an interpreter and a car. I began to call, one by one, these pastors who left their names. I told them when I was coming to their city. I told them to gather up the local pastors who would want to be a part and I would meet with all of them. So every day or so, I would meet with a group of pastors. I would see how many people they had in their churches. I would see what kind of facility was there for a meeting. This was about fifteen years after the war so there still weren't many big auditoriums. Over that summer I set up about thirty-five crusades for Europe.

This was my first big trip abroad. I was shocked to learn about the different cultures and the different views on religion. I was raised in a strict Pentecostal home. There was no drinking, no beer, no mixed bathing. We couldn't go to the picture show. We couldn't go to the ball game. We couldn't go to the fair. I was raised so strict and I thought that was the way Christians behaved everywhere.

My first stop was England. I was meeting with preachers to arrange the crusades. I learned the meeting was delayed a day because all of the Pentecostal Holiness preachers and their young people were down camping on the beach for two days, mixed bathing! This was supposed to be the strict group! I was so shocked.

After my meeting with the English pastors, I crossed the channel to France. I stayed in the home of a prominent Pentecostal pastor. He didn't have a bottle of wine in the house; he had a keg of wine! I had a little taste of the wine; they almost poured it down me. It was my first taste of any alcohol. I thought I was drinking rubbing alcohol.

My next country was Germany. They told me there were three hundred pastors that were meeting with me to plan a crusade for Germany. I went to the hotel where I was supposed to meet with the pastors. I asked the desk clerk in my best German where the meeting was. She pointed towards a door, I opened the door; there was two or three hundred men in there. They all had the tallest stein of beer I have ever seen. I don't mean a mug, I mean a stein. I backed out of the room and went back to talk with the desk clerk. About the same time, the pastors had seen me open the door; two or three of them grabbed me and led me back into the room. There on the table was a stein of beer for me! We had a great service and made all the plans we needed.

While I was planning crusades in Europe, I had to stop everything and fly all the way across the world to India to plan a crusade there. When I got there I was taken to the largest Pentecostal church in India. It was totally independent with no relationship with any church in America. This church organization was one of many that was going to sponsor the crusade in India. I arrived on Saturday, but they wanted me to speak in service the next morning.

The church auditorium could seat about a thousand, but the town was so abuzz that an American was going to speak, people came from everywhere. They set up a tent with speakers to take care of the overflow. When my time came, I said my few words, I thought I did great. But I came off the platform and the officials met me, mad! "Don't you know that you committed three sins in front of all of our people!"

All I did was walk up and speak and then walk back to my chair! "What did I do? It has to be a sin of ignorance. What did I do?"

"You spoke in the pulpit with shoes on. Don't you know the Scripture? Take your shoes off, you're on holy ground!"

I felt so bad that I had offended them. But I wanted to know everything. "What was the other sin that I committed?"

"You wore a wedding band. You are supposed to be married to Christ!" That was not the custom in my country, so I went about things my way.

I am not sure what the third sin was, but I was able to prepare the way for TL to come to that city for a crusade. The next day, I went down to their church. They took me around the church. They gave me a tour. When we got around the back there were two great big buildings with a smaller building between the two. There were little children playing outside between the two large buildings. I asked them if this was a school. They said, no this is where they live. I didn't understand what he meant. He tried to explain. "We are very Christian like in the Bible. When you are saved you sell what you have and give it to the poor and you move into our church family. The women live in the dorm on one side and the men live in the dorm on the other side. The smaller building is where men and women come together. We have sex with whom God leads us to." Those kids were the offspring of those relationships. They do not know who their father is.

When I got home, I went to see my Pentecostal preacher daddy. I ordered him to sit down and not open his mouth until I was through. I told him the whole story of the mixed bathing in England, the wine in France and the beer in Germany. I tell him about the three buildings with free love in India. So I say to him, "I want to know. Where is it that God changes his mind? These are Pentecostal people. They speak in tongues, they have prophecy, and God is with them. Where does God change his mind? In the middle of the ocean before you get to England? Is it in the channel between France and England? Is it when they stamp your passport into Germany? You can drink the beer here, you can drink wine here, and here you can have free love! I don't want to sin before I get to the line."

He got real quiet. I was ready to fight. I had been raised in a strict Pentecostal home all my life. Now I had come across Pentecostal people who had some liberties. Finally he looked at me and said, "Son, I don't have all the answers." That took all the air out of my righteous indignation. I just sat back on my chair with astonishment.

Later we had a good talk. One of the things he said to me was, "We have to learn in our Christian walk the difference between rules and sin. The country club out here has a set of rules for their members, or they throw you out. If they break the rules, it's not sin, it's just the rules. The Church has a book of rules. If you break one of those rules, it is not sin. But they have a right to throw you out, if you break their rules." That helped me as a young man to rightly divide what was real sin against God, and breaking the rules of an organization.

The meetings in Europe were set up for Monday, Tuesday and Wednesday in one city. We would move to the next and begin the next day for a Thursday, Friday and Saturday crusade. We always skipped Sunday. The team came back. It had been about three months since the Austrian crusade. I hadn't been back to Tulsa. This was when I started collecting art. I would run across warehouses of stored art. It had been stored there for protection during the war. The Osborns thought I was crazy because when they got back I had seven pieces of 18th century art in my hotel room when they came back.

TL's son Skeeter, was in his teens and he would preach at a youth service in the afternoon. TL would preach at night. On the last night we would show the Black Gold film I had scored at Evangelistic Temple. The film was so vivid and so noted that the Red Cross turned out at every showing because so many people fainted. The movie showed the African ritual of female circumcision. It was a very graphic bloody scene. We finally edited it out of the film. Each crusade became bigger. Europe is a small continent and the religious world is all connected.

One of the biggest crusades was in Holland in 1958. It was sponsored by the Dutch Reformed Church. That was the first big miracle in its self. The first night there was a huge crowd, probably a hundred thousand people. There were a hundred preachers on the platform. The Dutch Reformed Church had selected the interpreter. The interpreter was a High Dutch interpreter, very correct and proper in an Old Testament way. TL was having a real problem with him. TL didn't think he was interpreting the words he spoke. So he set him down. He tried out another interpreter, again he set him down. He got a third interpreter, and set him down. Finally he looked out into the crowd and said, "Is there anyone here, who can interpret for me what has the spirit of interpreting?"

Out from the crowd comes this tall lanky guy named John Maasbach. He said, "I was raised in New York and understand English." He stood up beside TL and within two minutes they were preaching. Maasbach understood both nuances of the language and the spirit of what he was saying.

The next morning at the hotel, there was a delegation from the Dutch Reformed Church. They had a petition for TL demanding him not to use Maasbach to interpret. Maasbach was not a part of the Dutch Reformed Church. The next night before a hundred thousand people and a hundred preachers, TL read the letter that was attached to the petition. It said the Dutch Reformed Church forbid him to use Maasbach to interpret. Because he spoke "low" Dutch. TL said, "I want all of you people to know that I speak "low" English so I want him to speak "low" Dutch. Either he is my interpreter or we close down tonight. Which do you want me to do?" About a third of the preachers walked off the platform. The Crusade took off and became one of the greatest Crusades ever. That crusade became a film, *Holland Wonder*, that has been translated into over seventy languages. It is now available on DVD and is still being seen by millions around the world.

When they walked off, TL said, "Now we can have church!" The meeting was awesome after that. God would use Maasbach to become a great evangelist in Holland. Later John Maasbach's son would marry TL's granddaughter.

TL's kids were often with him and Daisy. TL's kids were about fifteen and thirteen at the time. We were in Europe with these crusades. There was an American chaplain there with kids about their age. One night, about midnight I had a knock on my door. When I opened it, the kids rushed inside. At that time in Europe it was common for people to set their shoes outside their hotel door. The next morning the shoes would be there freshly polished and shined. These four kids had decided it would be fun to move the shoes to different doors all over the hotel including different floors! They ran in my room because, they thought someone had caught them.

The next morning everyone was checking out. When I showed up at the desk, this lady went into a rage. "Your kids, shoes everywhere! Floor, floor, shoes, shoes!" I told her that she was mistaken. I was in a single room. With that, I paid my bill and walked outside.

Those meetings ended in Hanover, Germany. The German pastors were not too excited about having an American lead them in anything. We had a three thousand seat auditorium with a Swiss interpreter. The first night of the crusade the pastors were very upset. The next morning they met with me at the hotel with an ultimatum. They said TL could no longer take an offering in the crusades because these were all poor people. I went down to TL's room, showed him the letter and I knew what his reaction would be. We had been on the road for about three months. This was the last meetings of the crusades in Europe at that time.

TL came down to my room about three or four o'clock that afternoon. He told me good-bye, he and Daisy were leaving. He said he took his orders from God, not from any local pastors. I had to go to the meeting that night. I stood up before the packed house, told them what their preachers had done. I told them about the letter. I read it out loud to the congregation. TL's response was, "I take my orders from God, not from any group of preachers! If any preacher wants to preach, be my guest." He quoted Matthew 10:14 "And whosoever shall not receive you, nor hear your words, when ye depart out of that house or city, shake off the dust of your feet." He went on to write, "I have already left the city and shaken the dust from my feet. As far as I am concerned you are free to leave."

TL's response spread far and wide across Europe. The people in the meeting that night were upset with their pastors. They had come to hear TL Osborn and the preachers had run him off. He became known as the man who took his orders from God. We built a great office for TL Osborn in Germany from a crusade we didn't have, but became very famous.

TL Osborn was the master of handling the mass crowd. He was the man who, by his actions, invented the term mass evangelism. No one in missions had ever heard that term before. In those days they would send a white missionary to win a native one on one. He created a storm when he started sponsoring native evangelists and native pastors. We had all the high officials of a Pentecostal denomination come to Tulsa and tell TL that he could not support native people with money and call them native pastors or native missionaries. They told him that he couldn't do it because he was taking the power away from the white man! TL stood up, ordered them out of the office and went right on doing what he thought God showed him to do.

We were sponsoring 1600 native pastors and evangelists at that time. We had crowds in the thousands in many nations of the world. We had a representative from a major evangelical organization tell us that no one on earth could attract 50,000 people at one time to hear the gospel. But we did that routinely in many countries with the TL Osborn Ministries.

TL was the one who pioneered having Healing Crusades without laying hands directly on people. When big healing ministries started after World War II, everyone had healing lines. They would anoint with oil and lay hands on people. You could lay hands on people in a crowd of five or six hundred. But when there are thousands that is not practical. The crowds were too big for TL to lay hands on people.

TL was trying to understand how God wanted to heal people in mass. His logic was, if you had twenty sinners come, you gave them the gospel, and you made it clear. If they all listened, they all believed, and you led them in a prayer. If they prayed, that prayer from their heart and believed it, wouldn't God save them all? If you take twenty sick people and applied the same rules, wouldn't they all be healed?

We were in Puerto Rico. We tried to convince the mayor to give us a big ball field. But instead we had to start in a theater that sat only about seven hundred. The second night the crowd almost tore it down trying to get in. The mayor and the fire chief finally agreed we could have the ball field. The first night he still tried to lay hands on people. They almost tore him up and the platform down trying to get to him. We knew this wasn't working. The next night we handed out cards with numbers. But they almost tore us up trying to get a number.

The next night we ask the police to pass out the cards. We thought they would help control the crowds. But then we found out they were not passing out the cards, they were selling the cards. The next night TL did the first mass prayer for miracles. God had given us mass evangelism and *Mass Healing*.

While working with TL I was able to visit Paul Yonggi Cho's church in Seoul, South Korea. This was in the early days of his church. It was meeting in a tin building. The TL Osborn Evangelistic Association had several films by this time. We also had ten gospel tracts we used which were in several languages. He sent his son-in-law, Jerry O'Dell and I to South Korea to interpret the films into Korean. He also wanted the tracts and some of his books translated as well. Jerry and LaDonna had just married and were in Hawaii on their honeymoon. I stopped there and picked him up and sent her home. LaDonna didn't forget that for a long time.

We didn't know anybody in South Korea but we went there to do a job. We landed in Seoul on a Saturday. We decided that Jerry would go to one church and I would go to another to see if we could find a good interpreter. We had arranged with the American Embassy to use their recording studio to do the translation work. On Sunday morning he went to one church and I went to a local Assembly of God church pastored by Yonggi Cho. It was a small building with a tin roof. It would seat about five hundred. They still had an Assembly of God missionary there.

I just walked into the church and sat in the pew. There was a visiting speaker from the Assembly of God headquarters in America. Yonggi Cho was interpreting the sermon for the congregation. I was in the unique position of understanding the visitor while watching Yonggi Cho. The preacher from America was making the most of his opportunity. He was quoting poems, quoting hymns and generally trying to impress. I was listening to the visitor as he waxed eloquently, and also watching Yonggi Cho translate. Soon I realized that Yonggi Cho was not preaching the same sermon as the American. When they gave the altar call there was a tremendous response.

At the end of the service I approached Yonggi Cho and asked him to go to lunch. He was open to the invitation so he had lunch with Jerry and me. When we told him who we were and why we were there, he was thrilled. He said, "Oh, I am so honored because I read one of TL Osborn's books and was healed. I want to do something for TL Osborn." We had lunch at the Chosun Hotel and afterwards completed the arrangements for the week.

At the end of lunch I said to Yonggi Cho, "Yonggi, I enjoyed your sermon."

He said, "You don't speak Korean!"

I said, "No, I don't speak Korean but I know you didn't preach his sermon."

He said back to me, "My people needed the gospel, they didn't need poems! I had to give them the gospel."

To this day when I see him he reminds me that I don't speak Korean and I remind him that he didn't preach that American's sermon. We worked all week and got everything accomplished that we wanted. Today if you watch those films in Korean, you will hear the voice of Paul Yonggi Cho.

I was privileged to put TL Osborn's films, books and tapes in over fifty languages of the world. Today they are in over seventy languages. But many things happened while we were recording the services and making the films. TL sent me to get a Nagra recorder. It was the first portable sync recorder that would sync with the camera. It was made in Switzerland. He told me to go get one. We couldn't order them. We couldn't get one because they were months back ordered.

After visiting for a while he took me outside to the manufacturing room about the size of a bedroom. This recorder was so popular that NBC had one, ABC had one, and everybody wanted one. Edward R. Murrow had just got one. These were invented by Stefan Kudelski. He was Polish but lived in Switzerland.

I walked into Mr. Kudelski's home in Cheseaux-sur-Lausanne. I told him we admired his recorder and I needed one because we were about to go to India. I had come after a recorder. Mr. Kudelski said, "Sir, do you know there is a several month waiting list? I have orders from all the major networks."

I said, "I don't care a hoot about the networks, I want mine"!

He said, "Do you know they cost three thousand dollars"?

I said, "Yes sir I brought the money."

He took me out into the workshop which was about the size of a bedroom. They made one recorder a week in this tiny room! He said, "Well, this one goes to NBC, but I can delay that. Take this one with you." God had moved us to the head of the line again!

It was my responsibility to do the recording during the filming of the Crusades. In other words I pushed the button at the right time. Sunday afternoon, we were recording the major sermon for the *Athens of India* film in Madurai. There was a hundred thousand people there. It was very very hot. I was on the platform sitting close to the edge, with the recorder in front of me. You had to punch the button and turn the knob to record at just the right second. If you missed it, you weren't recording you were playing. The film cameras start, TL starts his sermon, and I look down and nothing is recording. The light wasn't on. I realized it. I began to psst, psst, to get TL's attention. I finally get his attention and I whisper loudly, "Start again Rev!"

He looked me real funny. In front of the hundred thousand people and two filming cameras he started over and I got it recording this time. The service went great. The hundreds of healing testimonies were tremendous for the film.

After the service we went back to our rooms at the English Club. We walked in and I can tell he is upset. TL says, "I don't understand. How anyone with a college education? As educated as you are, as intelligent as you are, doesn't have sense enough to punch the button at the right time!"

One night we were traveling and we landed in Kenya about midnight local time. We had been traveling by old prop airplanes. Because we were so late, the airlines put us up in a hotel. The hotel had fourteen cabins. They were in a semi-circle with the office at one end. When I got to my room all it had in there was a small chair and a bed so small I hung off on all four sides. When I went to the restroom before going to bed, the only thing in the restroom was a hole in the floor and a wash bucket. Over my steel cot was frame made of two by fours to stretch the mosquito net over me. I lay down on the bed and tucked in the mosquito net on all four sides.

Just seconds later there was a knock on the door. I get up and go to the door and shout, "Who is it?" This is Africa at two o'clock in the morning; you just don't open the door in the middle of the night.

It was TL's son-in-law Jerry. He was standing at the door with this little mattress pad, mosquito netting and suitcase. "I'm not going to sleep down there by myself!"

Now Jerry was a grown man with a wife. He was no kid. I tell him that I am hanging off all four sides of the bed now. There is no way I am sharing that bed with anybody and I am certainly not going to sleep on the floor. He said, "Put me under the bed!"

He comes in and lays his mattress pad under my bed. We carefully lay the mosquito net around his mat. He lies on his mat under the bed. I carefully lay on my mattress pad above him. Then came another knock on the door. This time it is Cecil Clark, our engineer. He was standing there with his pad, mosquito net and suitcase. "I am not going to stay down there by myself!"

I tell him, I have Jerry under the bed and I am not going to share my bed with anyone! He says, he will share the space under the bed with Jerry. Soon I had Jerry hanging out one side of the space under the bed and Cecil hanging out on the other side. We have mosquito net spread out everywhere like a tent.

By this time it is three o'clock in the morning. We crash and sleep the sleep of the dead. The bad ending to this story is that Jerry was not totally covered by the netting. He was bitten by a mosquito. As a result he contracted malaria.

The next morning, we loaded our van and drove over a hundred miles into the jungle of Kenya. An Elim missionary from England had a lovely compound. He allowed us to hang quilts around his garage and create a proper sound studio for translation of TL Osborn's films into several dialects of Kenya. The missionary would bring different interpreters each day and the three of us slept in a bedroom in his house.

I will always remember the first breakfast. He gave us a written schedule. Arrive at breakfast table at 7:55 a.m., eat in perfect silence until 8:30 a.m. because BBC news of the world was on. That was their contact to the outside world. At ten we would come in for tea, twelve for lunch, one back to the studio, three for tea, three-fifteen until five. We had prayer meeting and dinner at six. Each of us was given a time for a shower as his handyman had to bring water from a heated kettle and put in our tub. At night, Jerry's malaria fever would come up. We would have to get up in secret and bathe him in cold water until his fever would go down. We would sleep a few hours, get up, and record the entire next day. After four days with this wonderful missionary couple who had given their lives for the gospel. We left without them ever knowing Jerry had malaria.

One morning my urine passed black. I thought I had black water fever. I remembered that one of the Osborn's children almost died from black water fever. I told no one. I kept it a secret. We left the next day for our journey back to the capital. I went to the home of a missionary friend of my father. He immediately asked if I was taking my malaria pills. I told him I took them religiously every morning. He asked to see my pills. I showed him. He started laughing. These are the new pills and you only take them once a week. "You have killed every mosquito in the country!" What a relief I didn't have black water fever.

While we were waiting at the airport in Nairobi, my father got off of a plane from Johannesburg. We had an hour to visit with him. We all went out in front of the airport and took a picture of the four of us. We were immediately arrested because it was against the law to take a picture at the airport.

We helped Jerry on the airline. We landed in Johannesburg, South Africa on Saturday afternoon. Jerry was scheduled to preach Sunday morning at a native local church. He was determined. He felt God would heal him during his sermon. God confirmed it and healed him instantly during the sermon. We set up a studio and recorded several dialects.

I was just a fairly young preacher's kid when I worked for the Osborn ministry. I would go all over the world to set things up for crusades. I was in a tribal area in Africa. The women did not wear any clothing above the waist. They wore a type of skirt from the waist down. This made it shocking for me to walk through the village while all the women were topless. There were often one or two babies nursing at the breast. But by the time I got the platform built, the lights and PA hooked up, I was beginning to get used to it. At least I was over the shock.

The crusade starts. TL walks up onto the platform. I had already opened the service, done my part. Daisy had done her part. Daisy introduces TL and he walks up to the pulpit. There was a native interpreter to one side of him. He looks out over acres of breasts. I am sitting next to Daisy. He starts his sermon. I could tell he was having a hard time. He would say a word or two, the interpreter would translate and then he would stop. Finally he turned around and faced Daisy and me and said, "It is sure hard to keep your mind on the Lord!"

We had a recording session in Liberia. We were staying as guests of some American missionaries in their spacious compound. They had two guest houses behind their main home. Jerry, Cecil and I stayed in one. Our restroom was a nice outhouse about a hundred feet from the door. Our shower was a bucket hanging from a tree with lots of holes in it. We would take a bucket and dip water out of the cistern barrel that caught the rainwater. The three of us stripped down, filled our bucket and poured it in the tree bucket. The three of us stood under it and tried to get wet. We soaped up and with a nice breeze blowing it was comfortable. Then we would take turns and get a fresh bucket of water, pour it in the tree bucket and rinse off. We had a refreshing rinse.

I noticed out of the corner of my eye, the curtain move from the adjoining guest house. I didn't know anyone was there. But all of the sudden I knew somebody was watching three naked guys take a shower under the tree bucket. I didn't tell the guys. I kept my back to the guest house window. After several trips to the barrel we finally finished our shower. We jumped up and down to dry off and we ran back to our cabin. I still said nothing.

That evening when we went into the main house for dinner, they sat us at a big table. They introduced us to the two other guests, two life-long women missionaries. They really smiled at us. Finally it dawned on Jerry and Cecil that they were the residents of the cabin next door and may have seen our shower. That night I confirmed it. They almost beat me up.

When we were filming the TL Osborn film, *Filipino Passion*, the missionaries told us about a lost tribe up in the mountains. So our film crew, Roger King, Baker and I and two missionaries got on a Filipino bus. It was open air. There were chickens and pigs in small wooden cages under the seats. It took us a whole day to cross that island on the bus. Every couple of hours there would be rest stop. The men would get off of the bus and go behind the trees on one side, and the women would go behind the trees on the other side.

We got to the end of the road. One of the missionaries had made arrangements for us to sleep in one of the churches the TL Osborn ministry helped to build. The ministry had built churches all over the world. The church was located on the beach. We were going to sleep in one of the Sunday school classrooms. By the time we got there, we looked like dirt because of the trip. The missionary said, "We'll go to the classroom and take off our dirty clothes. It will be dark in a little bit, and we will dart off to the ocean and clean off."

So we did. The five of us ran stark naked into the ocean. While we were in the water he said, "To rinse off the salt from the ocean, there is a faucet of fresh water on the side of the church. I put a bucket up there. We will fill the bucket with fresh water and pour it over our head."

This seemed like a good plan. So the five of us walked to side of the building, filled the bucket with fresh water and began to rinse the salt water off of each other. It was brotherly love and camaraderie of the first order. About the time it became my turn, around the corner came the ladies auxiliary. They had the task of bringing our dinner to us. We all turned inward towards each other and formed a short circle. It just so happened that I had the bucket and so I held it in a strategic place. The ladies walked past us, waved and spoke and walked on like nothing was unusual. We finished and got back to the Sunday school classrooms and got our clothes on.

The next day, we get on three outriggers, old fashioned outriggers. We go to another island. We get on another bus. We repeat the day. We stay at another church that night the ministry had built. We were going to bathe in the ocean again. The native pastor told us we would have to float out over the water for a hundred feet or so because there was coral that could cut our feet. So we floated out past the coral and began to bathe.

While I was out there, I noticed a big starfish. I wasn't sure what it was, but I had seen them in the marketplace. They were quite expensive as a souvenir. It looked dead to me floating on the water. I thought, *wow I got me a souvenir*. Oh, by this time we had bathing suits, for our modesty. I reached down and picked up the starfish. I held it and knew it was dead. When we got ready to float back, I wanted this starfish, so I just reached in and placed it in my swim suit.

By this time the kids had built a little bonfire. The ladies were preparing our dinner. There were kids everywhere. When we got to shore I reached in my bathing trunks to take the starfish out. That's when I discovered it wasn't dead! It attached itself to my body. A starfish has tentacles, which had suctioned itself to me. I immediately tried to pull it off. But the harder I tried the tighter it held on. I got really upset. I drop my trunks to my ankles and people were coming from everywhere to try to help me. Everyone was trying to pull the starfish off, but no one had any success. Finally, one of the little kids began to nod his head that he knew what to do. He got a stick, put the end of it in the fire, got it red hot, walked over and placed the hot stick on the head of the starfish. It fell to the ground, leaving me standing in front of everyone, naked. I reached down, pulled up my trunks and had dinner.

At the end of the second island was a small church supported by TL Ministries. They were very nice. We were able to sleep in a Sunday school room and the ladies fed us that night. The next day, we get in other outriggers to go to the third island where the Lost Tribe was supposed to be. As we began to go close to that island, our guides explained the outriggers could not go all the way to the shore. We needed to place everything on top of our head and walk to shore. So one by one, we stripped off our clothes, because the salt water would make them unwearable, and placed the equipment and clothes on top of our head.

The first guy to get out of the outrigger was Rogers King. He had his clothes, the camera and a tripod on top of his head. He was about six foot six, so everything stayed dry. When he got to shore, he set up the camera with the tripod and aimed it back towards the outriggers. We assumed the camera was not turned on, but we were wrong. I was the last guy out of the boat. The water was about four feet deep or so. I had my clothes and more equipment on my head. He was filming everyone walking out of the water and onto the shore. Every step we took, the water became more shallow, and more of our body was on display. He never said anything about the camera being on as we walked onto the beach.

We still had to walk up the mountain. Everyone knows about my trouble walking but they hired some natives to help me. There were no paths, so we walked up the creek bed. The missionary went first so he could talk with the chief and get permission to take pictures. They were all so thrilled! The men had on a G-string type of clothing and the women had their upper body clothed as well. The missionary had prepared them for our coming, so they had a hut ready for us to sleep in. So we started filming.

As we began to be around them, we noticed something. This was something I had never encountered anywhere else in the world. When one of the men needed to relieve himself, he would go outside the group, find a tree, place one leg as high up the trunk of the tree as he could, and water the tree. Their foot would be almost as high as their head. I don't know how they got their foot so high.

I told the cameramen, "Guys, this is their custom. When you got to go, put your foot as high as you can and water the tree. If you don't, people won't know what you're doing and you will attract a crowd. If you put your foot on the tree, no one will even notice you."

We had one cameraman from Arkansas. While we were filming he said, he needed to go, he would be back in a minute. After a few minutes, he came back, shaking his head with spots all over his clothes. He said, "I started to urinate. I didn't put my foot on the tree. Sure enough, in just a minute, kids began to surround me. So I decided to put my foot on the tree to make them go away. I got my foot up the tree and all the kids lost interest. But I lost my balance, fell backwards and created a fountain all over me." We made him go down to the creek and wash himself. We couldn't stand the smell.

We all slept in a hut. It was so small we all had to sleep fully clothed on our sides facing the same direction. If someone got uncomfortable, they would signal and everyone would turn over. Now in the jungle you create a lot of camaraderie. The next morning we got up and knew we had to find somewhere to have a bowel movement. We grabbed our precious toilet paper and went out into the jungle. As luck would have it, we found a tree that had fallen in a storm or something. Trying to have a private moment, we each dropped our pants and placed our buttocks over the log. We still were talking back and forth, making the plans for the day. About that time, big tall Rogers Keene, a little pig came up behind him and poked him in the backside. He jumped straight up in the air, the change in weight sent the log rolling, and we fell over in our own mess. We had to all get up and walk down to a mountain stream and bathe.

There are stories every day when you are out in the jungle like that. You get up every morning with certain things in mind. You have to ask yourself. *What are you going to eat? Where are you going to sleep? Where are you going to do your morning constitutional? Where are you going to relieve yourself two or three times during the day?* All of those events will create memories of the trips.

TL would write down the stories of the many people saved and healed in the crusades. This was what he told the people who supported him and made everything possible. I remember the stories of how we made films in the third or even fourth world countries. We made films in the most primitive of circumstances. Every day was a story. It was not uncommon for us to be island, canoe trip, island canoe trip and island canoe trip. We would cross an island by jeep or even mule, get in a canoe and paddle to the next island and repeat the process.

One time TL Osborn gave three vehicles to missionaries in South America. It was two Jeeps and an International Scout. The crusade was to be in Tegucigalpa. So we had to drive those three autos down. In those days you couldn't easily ship things like that. Besides, we wanted to see the presentation to the missionaries. So I was designated to be the chief driver because I knew how to get through the borders. TL Osborn's nephew, Gary Osborn and his son-in-law, Jerry Odell drove the other two Jeeps. It's a real problem getting autos through those country borders down there.

We get down close to the border with Mexico about four o'clock in the afternoon. I tell the guys we are going to the motel and go to bed. We are going to get up at two o'clock in the morning and cross the border. We are not going during this rush hour. If we try to cross now we will never get through. If we go through now the "chiefs" will be there. They thought I was a little crazy but we went to the motel.

We got up at two to cross the border. I told the guys to give me their passports. I took a twenty dollar bill and put it in each passport. We were told it would take six hours to get three cars through the border. I took the three passports to the first window with the money inside. Boom, boom, the money was gone. Boom, boom, he stamped the passports and handed them back.

I had to go to three windows. So I reached in my wallet and got out three more twenty dollar bills. I went to the second window, *boom, boom,* the passports were stamped and handed back. The third window was no different. Then there were guards on our trucks. I went out, shook his hand with a twenty dollar bill inside, told him we needed to go. He was more than happy to help us and we were through the border.

We got through the border in less than thirty minutes. When we got to the southern border of Mexico we had to cross the next border. They wanted to make certain we didn't stay in the country so they sent an armed guard with us. He would stay with us until we got to the border leaving the country. I must confess I have a little "mean" streak in me. I wasn't happy they made us take the guard with us.

He was riding in the jeep with me, sitting in the passenger seat. He was sitting with a great big rifle, almost too big to get in the Jeep. I don't know much Spanish, just my high school Spanish, so we didn't have much conversation. It was a warm afternoon and time for his siesta, soon he is asleep. He was sound asleep. I was going a pretty good rate of speed and I threw on my brakes. The gun hit the windshield, his head hit the gun and he jumped like someone was attacking him. I felt ashamed but I admit I thought it was funny. He was happy to get out when we got to the border.

We finally got down to Tegucigalpa. TL and Daisy flew down and we presented the three vehicles to the missionaries. T.L loved the International Scout. He thought it was a much better vehicle than the Jeeps. He and Daisy were going to take the Scout and go see another missionary. Everyone came outside to bid TL and Daisy good-bye. They were nearly surrounded by people. One of the missionaries looked at me and asked, "Can your boss take a joke"?

I said, "Try it."

He said, "I have a new gizmo I am going to plant in the exhaust of the Scout. When he tries to leave it will be like the whole engine is going to fall apart. It will make just a terrible noise."

I said, "Try it." I made the mistake of not telling our engineer Cecil Clark. Cecil traveled with us all over the world filming the crusades. He was from Arkansas originally but we found him working for KRMG in Tulsa as an engineer.

There are eight or ten of us outside around the Scout. We are telling them good-bye and TL reaches down and turns the ignition. The car fires up and immediately begins to jump and dance all around. We begin to tell him this is this Scout. The car he wanted and it runs like this. He should have driven the Jeep. It was sounding horrible. He turned it off. He waited a minute and turned it back on. The noise was as bad as ever. Cecil jumped up, told TL to pop the hood. He told him to start the car again. He does, Cecil tells him the problem is not in the engine but in the tail pipe. He goes to the back of the car and pulls the device from the tail pipe. The car immediately becomes normal. TL was not pleased at all. He did not see the humor in the joke. But everyone enjoyed the joke.

The next day Jerry O'Dell and I had been out in the bush all day. We were staying in a little native hotel. When we walked in the lobby we were covered with dirt. I know the clerk saw us. She said to us, "Boys, we have a wonderful hot mineral bath waters and massage down stairs."

This sounded great to us. We go down stairs and there are two great big Indian boys. They were really big and muscular. They striped us off and put us in this horse tank. The mineral water was very hot. We sat in there until we were almost prunes. Then they pulled us out and placed us on two big concrete slabs and started massaging us. They beat the whack out of us. They went up our sides, our legs, our back; I thought they were going to beat me to death. As I lay on my stomach, they started massaging up my legs. One hand went right up my backside. I didn't know what to do, I was just paralyzed. I didn't say a word. About that time the other guy must have done the same thing to Jerry because he said, "There go my hemorrhoids!"

We got off the table. They beat us so that we could barely walk. We were on the third floor. There was no elevator so we had to crawl up the stairs. We were so relaxed we felt like we had no muscles at all. We always wanted to go back down there and get another massage.

All of this was not new to Daisy. In the early days of their ministry before they had crusade teams, she was the setup team. She would go into a country and do the things necessary to build the platform, set up the sound and lights. She would take her kids with her and rent a small house or hut. She home schooled their two children, long before it became popular. She always cooked their food because it was cheaper and insured they didn't get sick. She raised her kids on the mission field. Finally, when they got older she sent them to Christian high schools to complete their education.

When I went to work for TL he had a very small and crowded office. If his ministry was going to grow and expand he needed a larger headquarters. I found some land near I-44 and Peoria. It had been an old farm. Most of the original farm had been sold. The farm house was the last part to be sold for development. I bought the land, hired the architects and engineers to make the plans for the new building. I needed $400,000 to build the building. So I went to Farmers and Merchants Bank there in Tulsa to get the money. I asked the president of the bank, King Bostock, for the loan. He said, "No, I'm sorry, we won't loan that much money to a church."

I went back to the office and spoke to TL and told him about the banker's decision. TL told me to organize and schedule forty crusades in the United States and Canada. At every place we go we will raise $10,000 for the new building. We are going to raise the money to build this building free and clear. We are going to start construction soon so we need to get started so we can stay on time with the construction of the building."

So I scheduled forty crusades across the United States and Canada. We would do one on Monday, Tuesday, and Wednesday and then start another one and go Thursday, Friday and Saturday. We spread the crusades over eighteen months. We didn't want to interfere with the overseas crusades. So we started construction. I went back to the bank and talked to King. I asked him that if in any one month we came just a little short, would he give us a small bridge loan to tide us over until more money came in. He agreed to do that. After we started construction I would call King every month and tell him, "We don't need any money this month."

I played the organ at each of the crusades. On the last night of every meeting, TL would have me place ten chairs on the platform. He would tell the crowd about the need to build the building. He said, "I am going to pray and then I want ten people to come up here on the platform, sit in one of these chairs and commit to giving a thousand dollars to the building program. You can either write the check tonight or give a hundred dollars a month for ten months.

This was a lot of money in the early 1960s. Each time he did this I would sit at the organ and pray with my eyes closed tight. "Oh God, please let ten people donate a thousand dollars so we can build our building. Let every chair be full!" Every time God was faithful and every month I called the banker and told him we didn't need any money.

While I worked for the TL Osborn Ministries I felt a tug on my heart to help the people in need I saw in our international crusades. Coming home from India, I stopped in South Korea. I came across some orphanages where they could barely afford to feed the children. I bought them all the groceries I could afford. But then I found another orphanage that needed food to feed their kids. Soon, I discovered that I didn't have the money to feed all of those kids. I was hoping this would relieve my obligation to God to help others. But of course it never did. It increased it.

When I went back to South Korea I heard about more orphanages that needed money because the workers had told their friends. I knew I didn't have enough money. To help everyone I had to get more friends to help me. But I didn't know how to do it. The Lord impressed me, don't go to the churches and take a missionary offering. I know the reason the Lord impressed upon me not to take offerings in the churches was because they were getting less and less open to outsiders coming in and raising money. The denominations didn't want "outside" missionaries to come in to their churches. But the Lord impressed me to go outside the church, to not touch the church. In fact, in thirty years I only spoke in three churches.

TL Osborn has been preaching the healing power of Jesus Christ for over sixty years. Recently he was in Thailand, more than fifty years after his crusade there. When he preached that crusade, most of the local pastors and missionaries didn't want him to come. But there was one preacher who really believed in him. He convinced all of the other pastors to open the door for TL to come for a crusade.'

On the first night of the crusade, there was a man sitting on the front row whose face was horribly disfigured. Part of his mouth was gone and his ears were gone. This man had been a leper. He had come down from the mountains in the north province where most of the lepers lived. All lepers were banished to that area. He had heard about the foreigner with the foreign God who was healing people. He came to Bangkok to attend the meetings. No one knew him. But he was healed! So when he was healed he headed back home. But he remembered the foreigner talking about a book. So he turned around, went back into Bangkok until he found a copy of that book, a Bible.

Fifty years later TL was in Bangkok. During those fifty years, the former leper had become a pastor. He planted five or ten churches. When he heard that T.L was going to be back in town he came to the service. This time they placed him on the platform. God did not restore everything that was taken, but his face shined with the presence of God. During those fifty years he had preached healing to the lepers of Thailand. God had healed them all! The nation of Thailand had certified there were no more lepers in the country. This was the legacy of TL Osborn.

In the early 2000s TL was in Gabon, Africa. He went to a grocery store because he prefers to fix his own food in his room when he travels. As he walked around the store word got out that TL Osborn was in the store. People began to flock him. In true African style they would come up to him and fall to their knees. Then they would grab his hand and stroke their face with his hand. There was a little girl who had been born blind, but now was an old lady, she had been healed at a crusade. There was a lady who had been deaf and mute, but decades earlier God had opened her ears and her voice. Now she stopped TL to speak the praises of God. It took TL nearly two hours to complete a few minutes of shopping. Everywhere he goes around the world, God allows him to see the fruit of his labor.

# BILLY JAMES HARGIS

I went to work for Billy James Hargis in October of 1969. I had consulted for him for about two months back in the 1950s between the time I worked for Oral Roberts and the time I went to work for TL Osborn. But I didn't work for him full time until 1969. The reason I went to work for him was because he was a world renown Anti-Communist. The Lord had laid on my heart to establish a humanitarian foundation. I told Hargis I would go to work for him, if I could open a missions department. He agreed. So that's why I went to work for him.

His biggest contribution to the anti-communist cause in the United States was his broadcast that won the suit regarding the fairness doctrine against the FCC. The suit happened because Billy James Hargis discussed a book by journalist Fred J. Cook, *Goldwater: Extremist on the Right*, on his radio program. His Christian Crusade program was broadcast over WGCB in Red Lion, Pennsylvania. Cook sued the radio station asking for free air time to respond to what he viewed as personal attacks. The suit went all the way to the United States Supreme Court. The Court voted 8-0 upheld Hargis and the radio station. If he had lost the suit it would like have destroyed the opportunity for Christian television as we know it in the 21st century. Without the suit, any time a minister said something that others disagreed with, equal time would have been required for the offended party to respond. This gained Hargis national attention.

After the suit the local station no longer had to give equal time to people of other religions. Imagine if every station had to give equal time to other religions when Christians bought time to spread the gospel. It would destroy Christian television as we know it.

I was the man raising the funds. Billy James preached at the cathedral and his daily radio broadcast. He like many others started on XEG in Monterrey, Mexico, preaching at night. The station could be heard across much of America. There were no 100,000 watt stations in America. The station was not far across the border. He was pastoring the First Christian Church in Sapulpa, Oklahoma, when he started on radio. When I first started consulting for him in the late 1950s, he was in a small frame house on Main Street in Sapulpa. During the thirteen years I was with TL, Billy James had built his cathedral with the pipe organ at 29th and Sheridan in Tulsa.

When I first went to work for Billy James Hargis they were in debt to the point of bankruptcy. The first day I worked there I had to take my personal statement to the bank and guarantee their debt to keep the place open. Then I worked my special delivery letter campaign. I asked for the Christian Crusade list of their best, most faithful donors. I mailed them a special delivery letter telling them of our need. We raised the money we needed to pay off the Cathedral. We always followed the special delivery letter with a magazine which had pictures of what we did with the money. You have to keep the confidence of the people.

While I worked for the Hargis ministry I obtained a license to create and build a radio station. The Christian radio station had an impact in the Tulsa area for several years.

# CREATING A CHARITY

While I worked for TL Osborn I had a heart for the needs of people. I would sit on the edge of the stage and watch people bring their starving kids to the crusade. Sometimes orphanages would bring their children to a service. I bugged TL about setting up a feeding station or a water station. One day I went too far. He had righteous indignation come up in him. Looking back on it, it was God speaking through him. He pointed his finger at me and said, "I'm doing what God told me to do. Why don't you go do what God told you to do."

I thought I was doing what God told me to do. But because TL allowed God to use him that day, that moment was the beginning being an NGO.

I had the understanding when I went to work for Billy James Hargis that I could create a missionary program. That became the Non-Governmental Organization. In the beginning some people thought that Billy James Hargis established it but I started it and Billy James was on the board of directors of the NGO.

When I left TL Osborn Ministries, I brought with me a former missionary to Japan, Jess Pettigo. When we started it I made Jess president and I was secretary-treasurer. I was the fund raiser and Jess was the field man to help set up the places.

When I decided to open the NGO I wanted to raise money for the ministry without touching the ministries I had worked for in the past. God gave me the idea to raise money through direct mail to organizations who were not known to be Christian. After

I got my paperwork identifying us as a 5013C, I got a non-profit mailing permit and went to work. I bought a mailing list from the Wine Buyers Association of America, the Racehorse Owners of America and a Tobacco Consortium.

When I talked with my daddy about how I wanted to raise the money, he didn't think it was a good idea. If you are going to raise money for missions you have to do it in the church. I talked with my pastor. He didn't like the idea at all. I talked to the bishop of my church. He thought the idea was crazy. But I knew the idea was from God and I knew it would work. I knew what God had told me. The idea was to purchase three mailing lists that could be used to appeal for funds to help provide orphanages with the food, clothes, facilities and other things they needed. I purchased the lists from those three different groups. In the late 1960s, no one would accuse these groups of having a Christian purpose or attend a church and give a missions offering. When I got my permit, we mailed an appeal letter to all three groups.

I got the idea for mailing from a trip I made to Washington, D.C. about that time. An invitation came out for two or three people who were active in the Young Republicans Organization to come to Washington for a meeting. I wasn't really that active in the organization but a friend of mine was and he invited me to go along. We flew to Washington. There were people there from every state. We met with a man named Richard Viguerie. He led us into a huge room. The room was really cool. There was a huge machine in the middle of the room. I thought it might be a locomotive. Viguerie got our attention and said to the assembled group, "This is a computer. c-o-m-p-u-t-e-r. I want all of you boys to go back home and go to your court house. Send me the name of every Republican who voted in the last election."

We were all curious. "What are you doing to do with them?"

Viguerie went on to explain. "I am going to place all of those names in this computer. This computer can do amazing things. It will write a personal letter from the President to every Republican in the country. The letter will say, 'Dear Lonnie and Betty, I want to come to your house and visit with you and your family about what we need here in Washington. The letter will be personally signed by the President.'"

We all thought this was a wonderful thing. Everyone went home and gathered the names and addresses he needed and sent them back to Washington. That is what transformed the Republican Party from the Country Club to the Rural Route. Richard Viguerie is still a friend today. That meeting took place in October of 1969.

When I got ready to start the NGO he came to Tulsa to help me with my direct mail appeal. We made our first mailing in March of 1970. In the first nine months of the charity, we raise over a million dollars net for the ministry. We became the gurus of raising money through direct mail for humanitarian causes. Each person that gave became our donor list. Then we began to cultivate them to sponsor the orphans one by one. We sent them pictures of their orphans and we built a base over those years. We had several sponsors that would give fifteen dollars a month without an appeal. The orphans became like their own child and they would send them Christmas cards and birthday cards. The office in Tulsa was the go between for all of that.

Everyone month we would send an appeal to new people. As they contributed they went on the donor list and received our magazine and newspaper. All of this helped us to grow very quickly.

Soon I was replicating what I did for TL Osborn. I sent my son, Royce, to Scotland to open an office. That established us in Scotland and Great Britain. I sent one of my employees, Christine Manning, to Switzerland. She was born in Austria and speaks German. She still lives in the same apartment that I rented for her those many years ago. So we raised money in the same countries we raised money for TL Osborn.

In 1971, we raised money to help in Bangladesh. It was amazing the response we got in Scotland. Bangladesh had once been a part of the British Empire. They had a tsunami which killed over three hundred thousand people. We sent an appeal letter to help those people. Our response was sometimes over thirty-five per cent. These were days before the computer in Europe. These were all hand addressed envelopes. We had a small minivan we used to deliver a thousand envelopes with the addresses to ten different women out in the country. When they were finished we would send the minivan out to pick them up and leave them a thousand more names and addresses.

When we opened in the United Kingdom, we went to the Post Office and asked for ten thousand stamps. They did not have that many stamps on hand so they had to order them. Word of that order got all the way to Parliament in London. One of the members of Parliament asked, "Who in Scotland needs ten thousand stamps? Are they planning to revolt against the government?"

The police showed up. They questioned Royce about what they were doing? He explained it was a ministry group trying to raise money for people in need around the world. After walking through the offices and seeing their non-profit paper work they were finally convinced. But the real thing that shocked them was when they were getting ready to leave; Royce told them he would need ten thousand stamps every Wednesday for the foreseeable future.

That wasn't the only time the local Scottish police came the office. When David Livingstone died, he wanted his heart left in Africa, what is now Zambia, and his body buried in the United Kingdom. When he died, they cut his heart out and buried it in Africa. Thirteen head bearers carried his body across the continent to the port where his body was taken to England. He was so revered there that the king had his body entombed in the main hall of Westminster Abbey, where normally kings and queens are entombed. To this day, when kings and queens are crowned in England they have to walk around the body of David Livingstone. That's why we used his name for the ministry. He was one of the most famous missionaries in the world when I was young.

The king wanted to honor the head bearers who carried David Livingstone's body to the port for transport back to England. He had a silver coin struck with the king on one side and David Livingstone on the other side with the name of each of the thirteen head bearers on the side of the coin. They presented one of these coins to each of the head bearers. Most of these coins are now in the British museum. They are very, very rare.

One day, the police came into the office. He asked the office manager, "Is this your David Livingstone coin?"

The manager said, "No. That's not our coin."

The police next went to the David Livingstone museum close to where he was born. It was only a short distance from the office. They asked the museum officials if the coin belonged to them. They also denied ownership.

The police came back to the office. They told the manager they would have to advertise to find the owner for a period of time, but if no one comes forward, the coin will be auctioned to the highest bidder. If you are interested, come to the auction and bid. When the day came, the manager called me, and asked if he should bid on the coin. I told him to go buy it.

He asked me, "How much do you want me to bid?"

I said go buy the coin.

He asked again, "How much do you want me to bid?"

About two hours later, he called back. He said, "You won't believe this, I bought it."

Well that was not a surprise, I expected him to buy it.

"But Dr. Rex, you won't believe what I paid for it. I only paid forty pounds for it. There wasn't anyone there who knew the value of the coin."

The next time I went over there, the office manager presented the coin to me as a gift. He told me the police said the coin had been found in the gutter. I have the coin still today. It says presented by the Royal Geographic Society of London in 1871.

One year the Canadian government called me on December first. They said to me, "Lonnie, you're the only one that we trust and can handle this much. We have six containers of dried milk worth millions of dollars. We will give the containers to you, if you will get them off the dock before December 25th. Because if we don't have them off of our docks, the legislature will not give our department any more dried milk. Can you do it?"

I have always said yes when I face situations like this. We figured out this was about twenty-two million cups of milk. I asked him where we had to go to pick up the containers. He told me. I hung up and called my accountant and asked him to find out what it would cost to ship these six containers around the world. I told him, we would ship one to Haiti, one to the Philippines, two to Kenya, and so forth. He calls back in a few minutes to tell me, it will cost $110,000 to ship those. Since it was the first of the month, we had no money. Also because it was the Christmas season, we had sent Christmas money to all of the orphanages so they could have a good Christmas. We didn't have any money at all.

I said, "God gave us these. I never turn down what the Lord send us. If by December 15th we don't have the money we need. You and I will go to the bank. You and I will borrow it, and you and I will sign for it."

That night, I went home and prayed to the Lord to tell me what to do. The next morning I got up and told Betty I was going to Washington, D.C. I was going to talk to the group who did our direct mail. I sat down with them. Told them what we had done. Together we wrote a letter. The one in the group who always kept us grounded, help write one of the greatest letters for direct mail ever. He said, "You need to have your money by December 15th.

Lonnie, we can't mail this letter. It takes five to seven days for the Post Office to deliver the letters and five to seven days for them to respond. I will take twenty-thousand of your top donors and send them a *special delivery*. They will have to sign for it."

At that time it took $1.07 to mail a special delivery letter. We would have to pay the Post Office more than $20,000 we didn't have to deliver the letters. But there was no choice. We sent the letters out. Within a week we had the $110,000 we needed, within ten days we doubled that. It was a God thing. That started the innovation thing of always sending special delivery letters. I'll never forget one of the letters we got back. I always quote it. The man wrote back and said, "Don't ever send me one of those d*** special delivery letters again. I am two miles from my mailbox. I went to the mailbox. The mailman left a note saying I had to come back tomorrow and be there when he got there in order to sign for the letter. I had to get up the next morning and drive the two miles. I got your d*** letter and here is your d*** thousand dollars!"

Direct mail attracted some unexpected responses sometimes. One day, one of our dear ladies in the office ran into my office waving a check. She said something I didn't hear very often, "Oh, Brother Rex do you want me to send this back? I am ready to send it back!"

I said, "What, what?" She hands me a check from Budweiser beer for $10,000. I told her, "Oh, isn't that wonderful? We get to spend some of the devil's money!"

Her demeanor immediately changed. She then said, "Oh, bless God, yes, yes, yes. I will go and deposit it right now!"

We met many awesome people feeding, clothing, and giving medicine to people both here in the United States and across the world. The Church of Christ in Indiana, the corn farmers, each of their members of their church had to have a "God's acre." Each year they took the corn from "God's acre" and they brought it to a special warehouse. Volunteers would come from everywhere and shuck the corn from "God's acre", place it in special bags and donate it to the needy.

One of the couples from this area who attended one of these churches called me one day. They were one of our regular donors. They said they had a container of corn and didn't know what to do with it. I told them I was going to Haiti and would love to take it with me. She mentioned she would love to go with me, so I said come on, and they did.

We took the corn, Indiana couple, and the pianist Dino Kartsonakis all to Haiti. We gave away the corn. Dino played concerts. Everyone had a great time.

A few months later there was a great earthquake in Mexico. Thousands of homes were destroyed but not many people died. They were just homeless with no food or clothes. I get a call from the Church of Christ. They said, "Lonnie, we will give you three forty foot trailer loads of corn because we know the Mexican ladies use corn. You have to handle the transportation."

Of course I told them I would take it. But I immediately began to ask myself, how was I going to get three truckloads of corn from Elkhart, Indiana, to Mexico? Then I remembered I had read that a member of the Coors beer company had become a Christian. I picked up the phone. This was one of the things I learned living in Washington, D.C. Always go to the top.

I called Coors and got hold of the guy I had read about in the newspaper. I told him the story about the corn. He said, "Lonnie, I'll tell you what I will do. I will send three trucks to Indiana to pick up the corn. I will truck that to St. Louis. I will put it on the Santa Fe trains because they go directly from St. Louis to Mexico City. I will arrange with Santa Fe to transport it down there free."

I told him that was wonderful. But I never thought of this. The next morning three forty foot trucks come pulling up from the country side to "God's acre" warehouse. Each truck with a forty foot Coors sign on the side. My phone was immediately ringing from Indiana because these people were just sure I was selling the corn to Coors for corn mash. It took me a while to calm them down. I had to get real religious. "God answered prayer. God sent the trucks. God did this!" It was all true but I had a hard time convincing these good Church of Christ people that it was Godly for the Coors trucks to move that corn. But they picked up the corn. They got it to St. Louis and on to Mexico City. We distributed the corn from the lawn of the president of Mexico. I later told Mr. Coors that if I ever started drinking beer I would drink Coors.

Years later, Betty and I were in Africa. We were driving a little Jeep and we were driving back into the bush to a little reserve. It had been raining hard all day. We came up to a creek. In Africa they don't always build bridges over creeks. During the dry season they will pour cement on the creek bed. When the rainy season comes the water will just flow across the cement bed. The advantage was trucks and large vehicles could still drive across. We came to the creek, water was really flowing hard. We didn't want to risk trying to drive across.

As we were sitting on one side of the roaring creek, a Budweiser truck pulled up on the other side of the creek. After a few minutes he got out of his truck and shouted at us on the other side. He said if we would back up he would drive across the creek. We backed up, he drove across. Once he got across he said that if we were willing, he would attach a chain to our Jeep and pull us across to the other side. We were willing. He chained us to his truck and pulled us across. We were so grateful. I told the driver, if I ever started drinking beer, I would certainly drink Budweiser.

# GOING TO POLAND

I got a phone called from the Reagan White House, the President's Assistant of Religious Affairs, Doug Wead. He was from the Assembly of God, the son of an AG official who had worked with my father. It was during the dark days of Poland. They still had a communist president, his name was Woiech Jaruzelski. He was a dictator general. They were in such dire straits that President Reagan wanted to do something for the people. He arranged for a shipload of dried milk. We had a great storage of dried milk in the Agriculture Department. But he didn't want it to go to the government because he knew it would all go to the army. He wanted to send somebody to photograph and distribute it to the churches, daycares and schools throughout Poland. I asked my friend Richard Hogue if he would send his video cameraman from his church to verify the distribution of the milk. We left for Paris so we could get a visa to go to Poland.

We landed in Poland late one evening. We stayed in a hotel next to the square in Warsaw. When we landed they had a car for us. There was a checkpoint Charlie about every half mile. They would stop the car, ask for credentials, look them over and send us to the next check point. We had to pass through several check points to get from the airport to our hotel. I didn't know it at the time but a correspondent from NBC was living in our hotel. We were happy because we would have at least one friend from the outside world. The room was so cold we had to sit on the radiator to warm it up!

All of the sudden we realized we had no car. We would have to rent one. We had no truck to pick up the milk. We knew no one and we had no interpreter. Then we heard a U.S. Senator had been arrested the week before for taking pictures on the grounds. That really had our attention. But, I always go to the top so the next morning I went to the president's office. They were so stunned to see an American that we were able to walk right into the office of President Jaruzelski.

I told him what we wanted to do. He said they had been expecting us. I mentioned that we had heard about the Senator being arrested. I said to the president, "I don't want to fool with all of that, I want a letter from you, so if I am stopped anywhere it says I have permission to video the distribution of the milk in your country!"

The president responded, "I am going to make it very easy on you boys, just give it to me. We will unload it for you and you won't have to worry about it. You can meet some of our people and then just go back home."

But I knew better than that. I said to him, "No, I have instructions from the White House that we are not to give the milk to the government because you will give it to the army and not to the people."

President Jaruselski looked at me, and finally smiled, so I went on. "I am going to distribute it to the children, churches, nursery schools, pre-schools, and schools, to the children. I brought a cameraman so that I could show that I did what I said I did. If you don't let me take the cameraman, I'm going to tell the ship to turn around and go back. Then I am going to go back to the hotel and talk to the NBC correspondent and tell him so the next day the whole world will know you didn't let the kids have that milk." He wrote me the letter.

I was very pleased about this. But I realized that I still didn't have a car, a truck, or an interpreter. Without those three things I couldn't distribute the food to anyone. But I remembered that

Poland was ninety-eight or ninety-nine per cent Roman Catholic. I decided to go to the head Cardinal there in Warsaw. I asked them to take me to the Cardinal.

I sat down with the Cardinal Karol Wojtyla. He spoke perfect English. I told him who we were and what we were there to do. He welcomed us so graciously. He gave us a truck. He gave us a driver. He gave us an interpreter. His office made all of the arrangements for the various times and places and told them we were coming. There was to be help to unload at every stop. Every day we would come back to his office at the end of the day and confirm the arrangements for the next day. By the end of the ten days we had a list of every place, how many bags we left at each school and each church.

We were there on a Sunday and the Cardinal made arrangements for us to go to church at one of the few protestant churches in Warsaw, a Church of Christ. Even then we had to go through several policemen outside of the church before we got inside for the service. They were identifying everyone who came to church. Just a little bit of intimidation by the government. But the people were very nice. We told them why we were there and they were thrilled. They even fixed a little lunch for us.

By the time we left, Cardinal Wojtyla was our best friend. I really enjoyed getting to know him. He was so down to earth. I could talk with him just like you and I are talking. About three or four months later I was shocked to open the newspaper one day and see that he was now the pope. I was so shocked. I thought that he had forgotten me now that he was pope. But soon I got a telephone call and I found myself and my wife in Rome.

# MEETING POPE JOHN PAUL II

I got a call from Father Gaines. He was a married former catholic priest. He asked me if I would go to Rome? If I would go, he would accompany me. He operates the largest rescue mission in upper state New York. I told him we would be honored to go, so he made the arrangements and accompanied us.

It was August, so the pope was not in Rome. He was in his summer residence about forty miles outside of Rome in the Alps where it was cooler. At first I was a little disappointed because I really wanted to go to the Vatican. But we went out to visit for the day. We were met by the pope's secretary. He was from Zaire. He was very kind and gracious. We were overly welcomed. I couldn't understand why this man was being so kind. I didn't know who he thought I was. He walked us all over that four or five hundred year old castle. It was one of the great experiences of our lives. There were so many great original art pieces from the great masters all over the walls. Every name you have ever heard of. The whole place was an art museum unlike any other in the world.

We finally got up to the top floor. This is the floor where the pope's bedroom is located. As he opened a window and we were able to look down over a garden, it was the most awesome scene. I can't explain the feeling that came over me. My wife and I were able to look down into this beautiful garden, and there was the pope on his knees praying.

The secretary said he will be up in a little while. Then we continued to go around through the hall and there was a door.

He placed his hand on the door and then he stopped and said, "Oh, I can't take you in there anymore. Because the last pope was murdered in here."

Later I made some inquiries. Pope John Paul I was only pope for 33 days. There were some major issues with the Vatican bank. Several million dollars was missing. Pope John Paul I found out who was responsible. They were the ones who murdered him. There was a book written, which revealed that but all of the copies were bought up and no more were printed. You can't find that book anywhere.

This young priest was so kind. He told me that he rode his bicycle over to the Charismatic Church every Sunday night. He was happy to tell me that. He also told me the pope was Charismatic. That was a big shock that day. But the bigger shock was about the pope's secretary. I found out that his uncle lived in a leper colony in Zaire that was sponsored by our NGO. The reason he was so kind to us was that he was trying to say thank you to us for caring for his uncle.

He told us during our tour that the pope had sent a message up for us. Rather than seeing us tonight, would we come back in the morning for his private mass in his private chapel at six? Of course we agreed, but we had to go back to our hotel, get up around four o'clock in the morning and be there before six.

Betty likes to tell the story that they had ramps in the castle instead of steps. I don't remember how many stories it was. Betty says climbing those ramps to get to the top floor of the castle, to the chapel, was like walking to heaven.

We got up to the top floor. The chapel wasn't any larger than our living room. He had mass every morning for the staff. When we walked into the room, there were just a few people there. The pope was in a prayer, kneeling. I will never forget the sight of the world renowned pope, on his knees praying. They took us to our seat. When the pope finished praying, he stood and greeted us in English. He told everyone what I had done for Poland. He embellished everything. He was so grateful for what I had done for the Polish people during those dark days. Then three priests got up from the front row. They had guitars. They began to sing, "This is the day, this is the day that the Lord hath made that the Lord hath made. I will rejoice. I will rejoice and be glad in it and be glad in it."

Lonnie, Betty, and Pope John Paul II

Lonnie and Betty guests of the Pope

Then Pope John Paul II stood and gave the mass in English in honor of Betty and me. We were so honored. When it was over the pope's official photographer came in and took pictures of Betty and I with the pope. We were told to go to the Vatican in Rome the next day and pick up the pictures. They were beautiful. We immediately went to Gucci and bought a book to put them in. Before we left the pope gave Betty a pearl rosary. He told her, "I only give these to heads of states."

He only gave me a more traditional rosary. But the greatest thing he did for us in appreciation for what we did for the Polish people, was place the name Lonnie Rex out to all of the Roman Catholic Embassies in the world. They were instructed to give us all of the courtesies they request. We used that for twenty-five years importing goods in India for our orphanages. We knew we could always use this to help others.

Later a Charismatic Bishop told me that he went to Rome for a meeting of Charismatic Catholics. The pope's secretary addressed the group and told them that Pope Benedict XVI had the baptism of the Holy Spirit. He told them the pope prayed in tongues, prophesied in tongues and sings in tongues. Now all of you should relax.

# MOTHER TERESA

Keep the joy of living Jesus ever burning in your heart and share this joy with others by your thoughtful love and humble service.

—Mother Teresa

Did you meet Mother Teresa before or after you met the pope?

❖❖❖

I think it was before, but I am not sure. Most people don't know this but the missionary David Livingstone took some African Christians to India over to Masik, India, about seventy miles up the mountains from Bombay. He established a church and a home there. The church is still there. In his memory I wanted to build a large boy's orphanage. We found the David Livingstone home. We found the David Livingstone church. We found people who could give us some of the history and we met descendants of some of the Africans he brought to India.

We built a large home there. It was a two story building with a wall around it. We wanted a director so we began to meet with various people. The newspaper editor of the Deli newspaper was interested in what we were doing. He was retiring, so I made him director of what we were doing. I didn't know but his wife was Minister of Health for India. So all of the sudden we had an open door to the government of India. His nephew became director of the home. Eventually we had over a hundred boys in that home.

I also didn't know that he was one of the best known Catholics in India. India has many religions including Moslem, Hindu, Buddhist, as well as other religions. With him being one of the best known Catholics in the country he told me one day, "There is a lady in Calcutta I would like for you to meet."

This was the early 1970s, I had never heard the name Mother Teresa. I agreed so we flew across the country and visited with Mother Teresa. This was before the world had ever heard of her. She took us to, what would become famous, the home of the dying. We came to this little building in what was the slum, slum part of town. Here were people who were lying on a concrete slab. They were lying on Indian mats. The floor was poured so their heads were slightly elevated. I walked through the home of the dying. There were so many they picked up every morning. The police would find them in the morning in the gutters or fields, Mother Teresa's ambulance would pick them up and bring them to that home. She could pray with them and they could die with dignity. That was her ministry.

I was thrilled with it. I said to her, "When they die what do you do? The first time in my life we walk into a burning gants. In one place there were bodies rolled in cloths. In another area were some priests building with wood. They would lay the bodies on the wood and then cover the bodies with wood. Then they had a ritual and lit the fires and cremated the bodies.

Mother Teresa would always have a Hindu holy man around out of the respect for the religion of so many. I took a film crew back to Calcutta to record all of the things Mother Teresa was doing. Went I got there with the crew the Hindu holy men met me at the gate. They told me, "You can't bring cameras in. This is a holy ritual."

They went on and on insisting I couldn't bring in the film crew. So I reached in my pocket and brought out a twenty dollar bill. I told them, "This is for your trouble. This is so interesting and American people have never seen anything like this."

The holy man grabbed the twenty and we walked in. As we were walking in he turned to us and said, "I will tell you what. You see that pile of bodies over there? There are four grownups and a baby. They were picked up on the street. We don't have the money to buy the wood to cremate them."

This was outrageous! I immediately said to them, "If you will go buy the wood, will you let us film it?"

He said, "Okay."

I told him, "Go buy all the wood you need." They left and bought the wood to cremate these five bodies. It wasn't a lot of money by our standards. I don't remember how much it was. They brought the wood in and built five tiers. They placed the wood, laid the body on top of it and then they placed more wood over the bodies. What was touching was there would be a hand out on one and a foot out on another. You could tell there was a body there. Then a Hindu priest would place a cloth over the tier. They lit the cloth on fire and cremated the bodies. We filmed the cremation process.

The cremation was very hard on Betty, especially the baby. To witness that baby being cremated with no one around to mourn was hard for her to take. She has never forgotten that day in Calcutta.

Later I said to Mother Teresa, "We would like to do something for you, what is your great need?"

"Oh", she said, "We need a vehicle to pick up the bodies. We have an old wagon but it is very primitive."

So, our office in Scotland found a right hand drive old ambulance. We shipped it to Mother Teresa. This was long before America ever knew her name. The last time Betty and I visited her, which was probably twenty years after we gave her the ambulance. By this time she was very famous. We saw that old ambulance in the parking lot. They were still using it after over twenty years. It looked like it was held together with bailing wire. We always felt very close to Mother Teresa. Every time we were in India we would go to Calcutta if we could and visit with her. It was such an experience.

Mother Teresa was instrumental in us meeting the actor Patrick Swayze. We were in Calcutta. We were staying in the Grand Hotel. We stepped into the elevator and there was Patrick Swayze and his wife. We asked them what they were doing in Calcutta. They were there filming the movie, City of Joy. We were the only Americans in the hotel with the exception of the film people. Every evening we would meet out by the pool and swap the stories of the day. We really enjoyed meeting Patrick and his wife. We had a great time.

Years later, he stopped in Tulsa to visit us. We had dinner with them. Years after that dinner, Globe Magazine carried an article saying he had cancer and if you would like to write him do it at this address. I sat down and wrote a tribute to Patrick Swayze and assured him that we were praying for him. A month later the letter was printed in Globe Magazine. We have such great memories of Patrick Swayze.

Lonnie and the Prime Minister of India

+LDM

MISSIONARIES OF CHARITY
54A A.J.C. BOSE ROAD
CALCUTTA — 700016

17th April, 1989

Lonnie Rex
David Livingston Missionary Foundation,
Box 232, Tulsa, Oklahoma 74102,
USA.

Dear Lonnie,

Thank you very much for your kind letter and prayers and giid wishes.

Pray for us that we may not spoil God's work but continue God's work with great love, that our lives remain woven with Jesus in the Euchar- ist and that we put the oneness with Jesus in action to the service of the Poorest of the Poor.

Let us pray for each other that in us and through us God be glorified.

Keep the joy of loving Jesus ever burning in your heart and share this joy with others by your thoughtful love and humble service.

*God bless you*
*M Teresa mc*

Letter 1

# WORKING WITH ERNEST ANGLEY

We had the great pianist Dino in our home off and on for a year or so. We were a place for him to hang his hat between concerts. One day he received a call at our home. It was hard not to hear the conversation. He kept saying "It's going to be alright Jim. Don't worry it's going to be just fine."

After a few minutes, he let us know it was Jim Bakker on the other end of the phone. Dino finally told us that Jim Bakker owned a television station in Canton, Ohio, but was in violation of the FCC for some reason. He was given a deadline to clear the situation but wasn't going to be able to do this by the deadline. Jim was just sure he was going to jail. He was beside himself. His only option was to sell the station by the deadline. I took the phone away from Dino and said, "Don't worry I will buy the station from you."

After a few minutes he got better control of his emotions. We talked a little more and began to work out the details. Royce and I went to Washington, D.C. to sign the papers. There were some final details to work out at the closing but after some negotiation we got the deal done.

Betty and I went to Canton to tell the staff that they now worked for us, not PTL. When we got there we found out there were no cameras, sound equipment, or anything else necessary to produce a television program. The only thing the station could do was bring programming down from a satellite. While Betty and I were driving Canton, Jim Bakker had given all of the equipment to another ministry. I was stunned.

Betty and I got in the car to drive to Akron, thirty miles away. I thought I would go see Rex Humbard. He had preached for my father the first time in 1946. We had been friends for many years. I was going to borrow some of his equipment. But when I got to the Cathedral of Tomorrow, I found out that Rex was gone to India and wouldn't be back for several days. At that point I didn't know what I was going to do. I had a new television station that couldn't produce a program. Within a month or so monthly payments were going to start for $25,000. I had planned to start raising money with a telethon but I couldn't produce the program!

Driving back I missed the Interstate entrance, so I got on the old Canton highway. As we were driving along we saw a great big cathedral. Soon we saw a sign and Betty said, "That's Ernest Angley's Grace Cathedral!"

I also wanted to see it so I pulled into the parking lot. It was about a three acre parking lot. In the middle of the parking lot was one car with the door open. A man was standing outside of the car talking with the people inside. We slowly drove around the church. We looked at the building. We saw the buses that were parked close to the building. But finally we came back around to that single car. Betty looked closer and said, "That's Ernest Angley!"

We drove up to the car and about the time we got to the car it left. There was Ernest Angley standing alone in the middle of the parking lot. Later he would tell us that he never walked outside of the church and talked with people in the parking lot. But there he was. I drove up to him and said, "Hi, I'm Lonnie Rex the new owner of the television station in Canton."

"Oh, I've been wanting to meet you!" he said as he pumped my hand.

It was about four o'clock in the afternoon. He took us inside to his office. It was at ten or eleven clock that night before we walked back outside. Before we left I had told him all of my problems. But Ernest said, "Lonnie, in the morning I will have my big portable television truck at your station. You can use it and I will leave it down there as long as you need it."

I said, "I want to do a telethon so I can raise some money to buy some cameras"

Ernest said back to me, "Lonnie if you do a missions night one night I will come and help you."

The next day the truck pulled up to the station. His technicians came as well. They set everything up so that it all worked. We had a barn for a studio. We had nothing. They brought me chairs and everything we needed. Then Ernest gripped my heart. On Thursday night, Ernest came with his choir, instruments including an organ and piano. He came down to the studio and helped me raise $400 thousand that week. The people were so gracious and kind. They packed the building out! This was the beginning of our friendship with Ernest Angley.

Ernest has been having a Friday night healing service for over forty-five years. You have to come early to get a good seat. They have the service in what used to be the Cathedral of Tomorrow that Rex Hubbard built. There is often a healing line around the building. The service starts at seven and usually ends about midnight. We attended whenever we were in the area.

One of those Friday night healing services Ernest announced that he was starting a local television program that would be airing five days a week. One of his strong supporters from Florida was going to be his co-host. I was sitting beside the new co-host on the front row. All of the time Ernest is talking about his new co-host, he is whispering in my ear that he is not sure he is really going to come. His wife says she is not moving to Ohio. I didn't say a word to anyone. When the time came for the prayer, he slipped into the line and told Ernest he didn't think he was going to do this because of his wife. At the end of the service, Ernest steps into the pulpit and announces that Lonnie Rex is going to be the co-host.

It was a great experience. Betty says we were great together. Ernest can be very serious with his people but I bring humor out of him. I would make things lighter. The people were shocked that I would ask him questions. I would say to him, "You sure got a twang. Where did you get that twang up here in Ohio."

I would ask him why he wore a toupee. I would ask him strange Bible questions. Soon people from the studio audience would come up to me with suggestions for questions. I would appear to not know anything when I ask questions then Ernest would preach ten minutes about the answer to one of the questions. I had a list but I didn't share it with him in advance. He bought two nine foot Baldwin grand pianos. Betty and would play a hymn on the grand pianos every day.

Ernest wanted to do some crusades in India. Because I had set up crusades in India for TL he asked me to be his crusade manager. So I set him up a crusade in Haiti. I worked with Max Manning there. I went to Haiti with Ernest, we had a great crusade. He was so impressed with Max that he made him his crusade manager there and they worked together for twenty-five years.

The next crusade was in Africa. I set that one up as well. It was in a stadium. We did two different crusades there. Betty and I were able to go on several crusades with him during this time. There was the Haiti crusade, Germany crusade, and then I went with him on a crusade to Africa. We had a big crusade in Kampala, Uganda. The prime minister of Uganda, Dr. Samson Kisekka, was a good friend. We spoke together at Oxford as well as Singapore. I had informed the prime minister of when we would arrive and where we would be staying. When we arrived for the crusade in Uganda, while we were checking in to the hotel, here came an entourage, drums, and the prime minister walks in. He walks straight to me, hugs me and we talk like old friends. Everyone around us was so impressed. Even Ernest himself was shocked the prime minister would greet us. That was a great crusade.

The most exciting thing happened during a crusade in Germany. I had connections in Germany that I had made when I worked with TL. I set up several crusades for Ernest in Germany. On the last night of the last crusade, he had a healing line. The auditorium wasn't very big. It sat about five hundred or so. The auditoriums were not that large in Germany at the time.

During the service I noticed at the back of the building there were police. We thought they were security guards or something. When Ernest started praying for the sick, the police came up and arrested him. They arrested him for practicing medicine without a license. They handcuffed him and drug him out of the auditorium in front of the crowd. They took him to an interrogation room. Two or three of us went with him. Most of his men disappeared. They ushered him off to jail. The next morning they told us they would release him on ten thousand dollar bail. I gathered up everyone in the tour group in the lobby of the hotel. I told them I wanted everyone to loan me a thousand dollars on their credit card. We would repay them when we got back to the states. We need to make bail. We put together the ten thousand dollars for his bail.

The next morning I paid the bail. I watched them release him from his cell. He looked pitiful. He had been praying all night. He was allowed to go back home to Ohio. He had to hire a German lawyer to represent him in the trial. It was to be held a couple of months after we got back. But the German lawyer was able to get the charges dropped. We never did find out exactly why he got arrested. I think it was because of the AD we ran in the newspaper announcing a healing service.

We were on his television show every day. Betty and I played a number on the dueling pianos every day. We had a fantastic time with him. He is so dedicated to the crusades. He never left his church except to the crusades. He takes his food with him. He fixes all his meals in his room. He never goes out. He never goes to a restaurant. He never eats food from the hotel.

Rex Hubbard left the Church of Tomorrow and moved to Florida. Hubbard's brother-in-law became the pastor. Since they moved to Florida they had no need for the television facilities. So Ernest Angley bought the television facilities. It was across the street from the Church of Tomorrow. The television facilities included a Buffeteria. It was the largest restaurant of its kind in Ohio. It could seat up to 1,200. It was a big buffet with three receiving lines. There was a large stage at one end where gospel singers would come and entertain during meals. It was really a great thing Rex Hubbard did when he built the facility.

The Church of Tomorrow had a seating capacity of about five thousand. There weren't very many restaurants built around the church. Everybody would go over to the Buffeteria after church for food and fellowship. When Rex moved to Florida, Ernest bought the television studio and the restaurant.

When we started the television station we already owned the facilities with all of the cameras and equipment. All we had to do was built a tower and put the transmission equipment in. When he bought the $25,000 license he already had everything he needed to start the station.

Two or three years went by and we began to hear that the crowds at the Church of Tomorrow were beginning to go down, fast. Rex Hubbard's brother-in-law resigned from the church. They put another pastor in but all that did was speed the descent. They got down to less than two hundred in a five thousand seat auditorium. Ernest's church, Grace Cathedral was on the other side of town. But Ernest told us he was going to buy Church of Tomorrow.

Ernest called Rex Hubbard. By this time Rex was in California. Ernest told him he wanted to buy the Church of Tomorrow. Rex told him there was a board meeting on a certain date and if wanted to buy it he should come to the meeting. Ernest said the Lord told him how much to offer for the building. There was a rumor that the City of Cuyahoga Falls wanted to buy it for a municipal auditorium.

In the meeting was Rex, their two sons, and Maud Aimee plus Ernest. The two boys said they thought the city would give them two million dollars or more. Angley said, "I have come and I have cash and I can arrange for cash. I will pay you $1,200,000."

The sons said they wanted to hold out for more. But then Maud Aimee stood and said, "I make a motion we sell the building to Ernest Angley for $1,200,000." Maud Aimee wanted the building to continue to be a church. She did not want it to be a civic auditorium. Then she asked for a vote. She pointed at each of the other three and said, "Yes, yes, yes, it is carried."

The next Sunday we attended church with Ernest Angley in the Church of Tomorrow. Ernest kept his old building. He turned it into a Bible school. It has been very successful.

# UGANDA

D r. Samson Kisekka, was a personal friend. We spoke together at Oxford and Singapore.. Dr. Kisekka was the prime minister of Uganda. He was a Christian, having been raised in a Seventh Day Adventist orphanage. The orphanage had paid for him to go to college and medical school. He had a private hospital in the capital, Kampala. I wanted to do something special for him to honor him as his friend. He needed an ambulance so we sent one to him.

The ambulance arrived in the port Mombasa, Kenya, with all of the appropriate papers. The authorities had notified my Tulsa office that the ambulance had arrived and all the papers were in order. But, they told me it would take seven weeks for the ambulance to be released. This made me mad!

I called Ryan, my grandson, and told him we were leaving for Mombasa tomorrow. Ryan and I went there to pick it up to drive it to Uganda. They agreed the paperwork was in order. But they said we couldn't have it. Again they informed us the ambulance would be released to us in seven weeks. We couldn't wait seven weeks! We were there to drive to Uganda, halfway across Africa. I walked inside the Port Authority building, found a set of stairs. I walked into every office until I found the one that said "Chief" on the door. I promptly walked inside. The man was shocked to see a white man just walk into his office without an appointment. I told him, "My name is Lonnie Rex. I am from Tulsa, Oklahoma."

The Port Authority chief immediately stood up, looked at me and said, "Do you know TL Osborn"?

I was shocked. In a million years this would not have been the response that I would have expected. I just had to ask him, "How do you know TL Osborn"?

"I was saved in his crusade here!" he said. The Port Authority chief began to tell everything about where he went to church, a Brother Sickler's church. In just a little bit the office was full of people who worked in the building who had been saved and filled with the Holy Ghost under the ministry and influence of TL Osborn. We just had a great prayer meeting. He made a phone call. Soon he was serving us tea. When we got finished with tea, Ryan and I walked outside, got into our ambulance and started our trip to Kampala.

It was a left hand drive vehicle from Scotland. Royce had searched for an ambulance until he found one. Uganda being a former British colony was a left hand drive highway system. It was a standard shift vehicle and because of my bad left foot I couldn't drive it. I had brought my grandson with me so he drove. He was left handed and could drive a clutch. Ryan was driving but I had my hands free so I could work the siren. We get on the highway but because it is Africa, a lot of people are walking on the side of the road. I played the siren all the way to Nairobi. We made record time because we didn't stop for anything and everyone gave us the right of way.

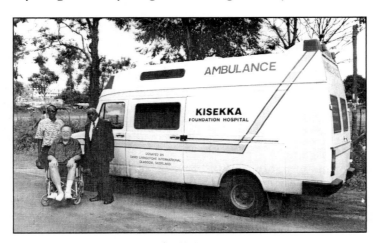

Ambulance

At night we would stay in the state parks. We had room to sleep in the ambulance. There was safety there. Sometimes we would rent a cabin in the state parks. So we drove all the way across the country of Kenya. We finally got to the border between Kenya and Uganda. There was a hotel there so we were able to get a good night's sleep. As we got into Uganda, every once in a while there would be a speed bump. We learned to slow down when we saw them. About two or three hours into Uganda, Ryan hit a speed bump too hard and it knocked our muffler loose. I tied the muffler up with a coat hanger. At the next small town we drove around looking for someone with a welding machine to fix the muffler.

While we were waiting for the muffler to be fixed, a nice looking young man in a suit with a dress shirt and tie, walked up to us. In good English he began to talk with Ryan. He asked Ryan where we were from and why were we there. Ryan began to ask him questions as well. He told Ryan that he was a banker. Finally Ryan asked him how many brothers and sisters did he have? He said his father had fifty-five children the last he had heard.

Ryan was shocked. He had never heard anyone with this many brothers and sisters. The young man went on to explain that his father had five wives. Each wife lived in their own hut. His father would stay in each hut, so many days a month. He said all of the mothers got along well.

After the muffler was fixed, we drove on the Kampala, Uganda's capital city with the ambulance. The ambulance was going to the hospital there. During the drive I had set my foot up on the transmission. I didn't realize the transmission was very hot. By the time we got to the hospital, my foot was beginning to hurt badly. I complained so Doctor Kisekka said he would take a look at it. The entire bottom of my foot was burned. The doctor peeled off a layer of burnt skin from my foot. In hind sight they probably shouldn't have. He put a cast on my foot and I was on crutches or in a wheel chair for the rest of that trip in Africa. We delivered the ambulance to Dr. Kisekka's hospital. We took a lot of pictures of Dr. Kisekka next to the ambulance and me in a wheel chair.

We spent the day with him on his farm outside of Kampala. He had the largest greenhouse I had ever seen. All he grew was red roses. Long stem and short stem red roses. Every Friday he sent fifty-thousand red roses by KLM airlines to Amsterdam to the international market there. There was row after row of greenhouses. The people who worked on the roses didn't have to bend down because they were grown in waist high beds. They could stand and trim the roses and cut the roses. They cut every day. Over in the processing area they had all of the roses laid out. Long stem, short stem, good and bad ones, all ready to go to cold storage.

From Kampala we flew to Zambia. It just so happened that Benny Hinn was in Zambia conducting a crusade. I was friends with President Chiluba as he and his wife had appeared at Grace Cathedral with Ernest Angley. He was a professed Christian. My wife Betty accompanied his wife on the piano while she sang. We attended the crusade that afternoon as the guests of President Chiluba. There was the two of us, the president and his wife, plus the bodyguard. We were seated in a special roped off section of the stadium. All of the sudden, Benny Hinn said anyone who wanted to get closer to the platform should come on down. Within moments the ropes were down and people were everywhere we. The bodyguard led us down a back way. We were able to escape the pressing mob with our lives.

President Chiluba was very impressed with Ryan. He asked him if he had ever bungee jumped? Ryan said no but he always wanted to. The president told his driver to take me and Ryan about a hundred miles to Victoria Falls the next day to bungee jump. Ryan was so excited. I wasn't sure what a bungee jump was. I had seen one at the fair. It dropped about a hundred feet or so. But the driver took us to Victoria Falls. There was a bridge which led from Zambia to Zimbabwe. The bridge is more than six hundred feet across. It is over four hundred feet to the water below. They put Ryan in a harness. They told him to jump out as far as he could because of the bridge. The fall with the bungee cord was over three hundred feet. It looked like he hit the water to me, but he didn't and he soon came back up. Eventually they pulled him back up to the bridge.

The next day we flew to South Africa to meet with Nelson Mandela. We were going on behalf of the International College. I was on the board of Armand Hammer's International College in Montezuma, New Mexico. Queen Noor of Jordan, Prince Philip of Greece and his mother Queen Ann, and Queen Sofia of Spain, all worked with us on the board of International Schools. It was my privilege to work with the International Colleges. Mandela was on our international board. Mandela was ill so we were not able to meet with him. I have always regretted that I wasn't able to meet Mandela.

# MY MANY DEALINGS WITH RUSSIA

Nine veteran's organizations had petitioned the White House to arrange an invitation for them to go to the Soviet Union. They wanted to interview Russian generals about possible Vietnam MIAs. The Soviet Union had petitioned Congress for some humanitarian aid. Congress turned them down. The Soviet Union agreed to allow the veterans organizations to come if they brought an NGO with some humanitarian aid. I was the chosen NGO. The government wanted to make certain there were no longer any prisoners of war left in Vietnam. They wanted to recover as many bodies as possible of soldiers left behind. We took with us about $200 thousand worth of antibiotics. We were among the first Americans to come to Russia while Mikhail Gorbachev was in power. He was looking to the west to help change Russia.

Everywhere we went there were three KGB agents with us. They never left us. They were either in our room, or in the other guy's room or outside in the hall. I became friends with one of the agents who always seemed to be around me. He was able to speak some English, so we could communicate some. We had a great time. He took me to one of the big communist camps and we spent the night there. They gave us all a eucalyptus bath. When we got out of the bath these big boys proceeded to give us rub down. I thought they were going to kill us!

They also took us to a local village. Most of the people in the village had never seen an American. We were probably a thousand miles from Moscow. But they wanted us to see a real communist village. We were led down the street to a house where the village baker lived. He baked all the bread for the village. We were all treated to fresh hot bread. Then they took us back down the street in another direction. At that house we found people who would pick berries and make jelly for the village. The next house was the family who raised and milked the cows. That provided milk and butter for the village. We had hot bread with jelly and butter to spread on it. We ate the whole loaf of bread. It was wonderful!

One night they gave a banquet in our honor at the headquarters of the KGB. Everyone had a glorious time. The vodka was flowing freely. The veterans from America and the KGB agents were very relaxed. I turned to the KGB agent with me and asked him, "Do you have a KGB file on Lonnie Rex upstairs"? He nodded yes. So I went further. "Could I see it"?

He raised his finger to his lips and said, "Yes, but you can't tell nobody." He got up from the table and came back with a file that looked about three or four inches thick. I opened it up and began to flip through it. I saw pictures of me going into the Russian Embassy. There were pictures of me in Africa. They had a complete biography of me. They knew everything about me. They had followed me around the world. It made cold chills go up my spine. I was stunned!

Several years later after the fall of communism, Boris Yeltsin became the president of Russia. After his term was up, he was succeeded by a former KGB agent named Vladimir Putin. He was the same KGB agent who had escorted me around years earlier. He remembered me. When he was inaugurated as president, he sent for Betty and I to come to Moscow to attend the ceremony. We were the guests of the Kremlin National Hotel. We stayed in Moscow for ten days. We were treated like heads of state. We were wined and dined the entire time. Our official host was the prime minister of Russia.

They knew I was religious. One day while we were having lunch I looked over to a priest from the Russian Orthodox Church and asked him, "President Gorbachev told me yesterday that we now have religious freedom in our constitution, the new constitution. Do you have religious freedom?"

He ducked his head and said, "The Baptist do. They take it but we are still a little too scared. We had too many churches confiscated and priests killed. But they have given us back now, two thousands of our church buildings that had been taken and placed into other use. But they are not all open now because we don't have enough priests. We have two thousand priests in seminary, but we do not have a Bible for each church"

I said, "How many do you need"? He told me and I told him "You did now. I will supply the money." It was a great opportunity to do something for the Russian people.

Gorbachev sent us to several of their larger cities. One of the cities was Yekaterinburg. This was the city where the U-2 pilot Gary Powers parachuted when he was shot down in 1960. They invited me to speak to the city council. This was in August and for the first time in seventy years they had a city council. When I spoke to the City Council there were probably two hundred people packed in the council chambers. They had all come to hear the American.

When I finished my speech I threw the floor open for any questions. The first question was, 'How do you handle freedom?"

I answered the question with a question. "Let me ask you this, how do you handle me being here today?"

He answered, 'We're happy you're here."

I said, "That how you handle it. One day at a time. Take what you're given."

When it was over this big, tall, older guy with a chest full of ribbons walked up to me. He said to me, "I am the man who calculated the rocket punched the button that brought down your Gary Powers. That rocket sucked into the tail of the plane.

By all conditions it should have disintegrated." Then he began to punch me on the chest, "Your God saved him!"

Later we went home with the mayor and had lunch with him and his wife and kids. While we were eating and he looked at me and said, "I am the man, who punched the button that shot down the Korean Air Lines Flight 007 that killed 269 people. I have to live with that. But I had instructions from Moscow." In one day, I met two people of history.

The mayor had a serious subject to discuss with me. He told me their city had been a center of manufacturing for their military. He told me they had one plant which employed twenty thousand people who made tanks. They had another factory which also employed twenty thousand which made rifles and guns. A third plant made refrigerators also employed ten thousand. He told me they had received word from Moscow that the war was over so they should cut back on making the armaments. He didn't know how to do that.

I told him that was simple but I had two questions. "Can you use more refrigerators than you are making"? He assured me they could sell all the refrigerators they could build. So I asked the second question. "Can you take ten thousand people from the tank factory and let them work the second shift of the refrigerator plant. Then let's take ten thousand from the rifle factory and let them work the third shift."

Then a hand was raised. "If we do this when do we sleep?"

I explained the concept of a second shift and a third shift. They didn't understand. I thought it was a language issue, so I worked with my interpreter to better explain the concept. But no matter how hard I tried, they never grasped the concept of a factory working three shifts a day. Finally we went on to something else.

The next thing they asked about was banking. They knew I had some experience in banking. They had heard from Moscow and had permission to establish a private bank in the city. This was one of the largest cities in Russia. They had never had a private bank. They knew I had brought training manuals from America that told how to operate a bank. The manuals covered everything from the bank tellers to the back office and everything in between. Finally they said, "We want you to be the president of our first bank."

I was flattered that they would want me to lead their first bank. But I wasn't sure why. I asked them, "Why do you want me to be the president of your first private bank"?

The room was full of KGB agents but they answered truthfully anyway. They said, "You don't understand. The Russian people have no confidence in the Russian government. We all have our money under the mattress, in the coffee can, or buried in the backyard. If you will become president of the bank, the people will trust us. They will pull their money out from their hiding places and bring it to the bank."

I said, "This would be a great honor. But with my other responsibilities, I would not be able to do it justice."

When I got back to Moscow, the governor of Belarus, the province where the Chernobyl Nuclear disaster had taken place, learned I had grown up in Enid, Oklahoma, the wheat capital. The government was just beginning to privatize the farms. The governor told me that he would give me ten thousand acres of their best land if I would come and bring forty tractors and forty combines. I would also teach their farmers how to raise the yield per acre from five to eight bushels to forty to fifty bushels. I told the governor, "I am going to go home and think on this. I don't think there is anything I would love more than to come here and to that."

I came home and called the John Deere Company. I talked to the tractor people and the combine people. I got quotes. I got shipping costs. I talked to the president of John Deere, told him what I was doing. He agreed to ship everything for free. But I had to go to Russia and commit myself for five years. I had to decide whether to go to Russia and be a farmer or continue to do what God had called me to do. I was riding down the highway in a motor home with some friends on my birthday. My cell phone rang. It was my friend in Russia wishing me happy birthday. He was there when the governor made me the offer. I told him I was turning it down. The governor was very, very unhappy.

Gorbachev knew I had owned a television station. He sent word over to the Metropolitan asking if I would join with him to do a telethon. They had just ended their Afghanistan war. They had withdrawn all of their troops. But what they had not done was inform the public of those who had died in the war. When the Russian soldiers died during the war their families were not told. When they ended the war they had to tell the families their loved ones were not coming home. Gorbachev was under a lot of pressure.

Lonnie, interpreter, and Mikhail Gorbachev

126

He asked me to do a telethon with him. It would last for twelve hours, from noon to midnight. He asked me how to do it since I had experience. I told him how we did ours. He gave me the navy band, the army band and all of the best opera singers in Russia. He and I sat there for the twelve hours, except when we had to go to the bathroom, and raised money for the children of the dead Afghanistan veterans.

We did have some problems. The people didn't have checking accounts. They didn't have credit cards or debit cards or any of that. They wouldn't put money in the bank because they didn't trust the banks. They couldn't send money in so they had to go to the local television station. For twelve hours we were on every television station in Russia by direction of the central government. The ambassador from North Korea to Russia watched the program. He wrote down my name.

When I got back to the Metropolitan Hotel, I had a note from the prime minister of Russia, asking if he sent a driver would I come to see him. Of course, I agreed to see him. The next day the driver came to the hotel and took me to see the prime minister. They ushered me into his office. After the door was shut and we were alone, he leaned across his desk and quietly said to me, "Do you have a *beeble?*"

Even though his accent was strong, I understand what he meant. I did indeed have Russian Bibles. Before I left the states for Russia, I had purchased ten Russian Bibles and I packed them in my bag. I had planned to give them as gifts while I was there. I had one in my briefcase at that moment. I reached down, opened the briefcase, pulled the Bible out and laid it on the desk. He reached across and gently picked up the Bible and held it in his hands. He then said surprising words, "I never see a *beeble*. I always want a *beeble*. My mother signed me on the church when I a baby." He was trying to tell me that he was a Christian. He took the Bible and placed it inside his desk. Then he called everyone into his office and we had tea.

As we were having our tea the prime minister said, "Dr. Rex, we have the greatest potato crop we have ever had." I knew that in Russia if they had a good potato crop that meant the people would eat that year. If they don't have a good potato crop there is a famine.

Then it looked like he might cry. The prime minister said, "It looks like we might lose half of the crop. Russia is a huge country. The potato fields are way up in another district. It is so far away and sparsely populated. The potato crop is ready to harvest all at one time. If they are not harvested quickly they will rot in the fields. We don't have enough people up there and because it is a huge crop there is no way they can dig all of the potatoes. But even if we could dig the potatoes, we have nowhere to store them. They would still rot. But even if they were harvested and store properly, we don't have enough trucks to move the potatoes to where the people live.

When he got through reciting all of the reasons they could not harvest these potatoes, I stood up, reached over, and just slapped the desk. I said, "Well, that's not true." People standing around me were amazed at the way I spoke to the prime minister. But I continued on, "President Gorbachev told me yesterday that the war was over." They agreed that was true.

I labored on, "You have the biggest army in the world. But they are all just sitting around us in the camps eating all of the potatoes. They are sitting on their butts doing nothing. Take all of the army boys up there. You have more trucks than anyone in the world. Put your soldiers in those trucks. Take them up to that district, dig up the potatoes, leave some for the people and bring the rest back to the army base. Take the tarpaulin off the army carriers because all you need to store potatoes is put a tarpaulin on the ground to keep the water from coming up and put one over them to keep the water from coming down. You will save every potato.

I finished by telling him, "I'm an old country boy from Oklahoma. That is where you get half of your wheat. I know how to store potatoes. Instead of having your soldiers here sitting on their butts eating potatoes. Make them go up there and dig them!"

The prime minister stood and slammed his hand on his desk. He said, "Come with me!" I followed him outside. We jumped in the back of a limousine. The driver immediately took us to the Kremlin. He led me to an office that said, USSR chief. We walked into the office. There was a great big guy sitting behind the desk. He wasn't sure what was going on, but he jumped straight up from his chair and saluted the prime minister with his hand shaking noticeably. The prime minister and I never sat. This was obviously not a social visit.

The prime minister said, "Tell the general, what you told me!"

I waxed eloquently for the next few moments as I explained the plan I had described to the prime minister. As I was talking the prime minister raised his hand in the air and firmly said, "Stop!" He looked straight into the eyes of the general, "I want the army moving in two hours. I want every potato dug up. Leave some for the people up there. Bring the rest of them back to the base. Take those tarpaulins off of those trucks and do what he says."

The general reaches down below his desk and pushes a button. Within a few moments, I was surrounded by the top generals of all of the armed services of Russia. The chief general looked at me, "Tell them what you told me." Now I raised my voice with authority. I again told my story to my fixed audience. When I finished, the general continued. He told them where their regiments were supposed to go. He told them to leave within two hours. With that, the prime minister and I got back in his limo and left.

That night I was back at my hotel having dinner with the Patriarch of the Russian Orthodox Church and his guests. During dinner I got an urgent call from my son Royce back in Tulsa. The first words out of his mouth were, "Dad, are you alright?"

I told him, "Yeah, I'm alright. Why are you asking?"

Royce said, "Dad, CNN, ABC and all of the television networks are reporting that Russia is invading some country. All the highways are full of army trucks, army carriers because our satellites can tell they are full of soldiers. They must be invading some country! But no one knows where they are going?"

I said, "Royce, don't worry about it. They're just going up there to dig potatoes. Go to bed."

Through my relationship with the prime minister I was able to develop a relationship with the Minister of Health. Through that relationship I was able to impact millions of people in Russia. I became known as the "condom" man in Russia. I received a phone call from a latex company one day. The man on the other end of the phone asked me if I could use some of their product. When anyone calls, the answer is always yes. Give me as much as you can of whatever you have. But he went on to say, "Now, you do understand I am talking about condoms?"

I replied, "I can use all you can give me. Give me a couple of hours to make some phone calls."

He said, "Well, I have four, forty foot containers. We think this is about 22,000,000 condoms."

I said, "Give me an hour and I will give you an answer."

I called the health minister of Russia. He was so excited. He told me, "The average woman in Russia has had five abortions. Where are these condoms manufactured?"

I told him they were manufactured in Camden, New Jersey. He said, "Dr. Rex, we have a ship in the New York harbor. If you will have them truck them over to our ship we will bring them to Russia for free."

I called the latex man back. I explained the situation to him. He was happy to send the condoms to the Russian ship in the New York harbor. In three phone calls I sent 22,000,000 condoms to Russia. They distributed the condoms to their clinics all over Russia. There is no telling how many abortions were prevented.

I developed a strong relationship with the government of Russia. I got a call one day asking me to come to Washington, D.C. to visit the Russian Embassy. I agreed to go. When I got to Washington they escorted me into a very beautiful reception room. They said, "This is the room where Gorbachev and President Reagan first met. We want you to know how highly we honor your visit."

I knew they had asked me to come to Washington for much more than to see a room in their embassy. I asked them, "What do you want"?

They said, "We have a very special request for you. You are the only person we trust to do this. We have just finished our war in Afghanistan. The crazy mujahedeen have captured two of our generals. We want you to go as an NGO to Afghanistan and get them released."

I said okay, because that was always my answer. If God opened a door, I always walked through it. I went to the Pakistan embassy and visited with the American ambassador from Pakistan. When I told him what I was going to do he told me an American cannot go into Afghanistan.

I told him, "I know an American cannot go but I am not going as an American. I am going as a NGO. I am going as a humanitarian. I don't represent the United States. If there are two men over there being held captive, I want to go get them." He couldn't believe me. But after talking for a while he agreed to make the arrangements for me to cross the border from Pakistan to Afghanistan.

I met with the mujahedeen. I wasn't sure if they would behead me; kidnap me, or just what they would do. The mujahedeen said they would not release them unless they receive certain things they needed. There was nothing unusual on their list. They needed some rice and other supplies. I could easily provide everything they asked for.

After my meeting with the mujahedeen I went back to Pakistan and called the Russian embassy. They called their embassy in Pakistan. They made all of the arrangement for the supplies. A few days later they met me at the border and released the generals to me.

About two weeks later I received another call from the Russian Embassy. This time they told me over the phone what they needed. "We have two of our government workers captured in Ethiopia. Could you go get them?"

Again I agreed. I knew exactly where they were. Years earlier the Russians had drove all of the Christians up into the mountains to starve them. I knew that's where they would be. I told them that I would need a plane ticket to fly to Kenya. The president of Kenya was a personal friend. He had given me five acres to build a clinic on out of his personal farm. He would give me a military escort across the border into Ethiopia to pick them up. I told them, "Inform your embassy in Kenya that I'm coming. I need a place to stay and use of a car." All of the arrangements were made but they were released before I went.

I received a call one time to go to Russia and educate their legislature, the Duma. They wanted me to speak to them about Non-Government Organizations or NGOs. They wanted me to tell them how American NGOs could help them in their transition from communism to democracy. I spoke to the Duma about NGOs. Later I would bring nine Russian governors to Oklahoma to meet with Governor Frank Keating.

Lonnie getting knighted

On the second trip with the various veterans organizations, something else happened which has impacted my life. I was knighted into the Knights of Malta. I was the only American to be so recognized. I was staying in a cottage on the grounds of the home of the Patriarch of the Russian Orthodox Church. They considered me to be religious. My grandson Ryan was on the trip with me. The Patriarch wanted to do a knighting ceremony. The Knights of Malta for the last two hundred years had been knighted by either the Pope in Rome, the Queen of England or the Czar of Russia. Since the Czar had been killed in 1918, the Patriarch was assuming that responsibility. The government had agreed he could do that.

Among the others were four top Russia generals, the prime minister and the governor of a Russian state. The Russian general who was knighted was the individual given the task of telling Gorbachev that he was no longer the leader of Russia. They knighted me for humanitarian reasons.

I was informed the night before that I was being knighted the next day. Across the big yard of the Patriarch's residence was a chapel that was built in the 9th century. There was gold everywhere in the chapel. I got the call about the knighting ceremony. I was honored but I really didn't understand everything involved at the time. They brought me specific articles for the ceremony; a robe, spurs, and a sword. I was later given a second sword as a humanitarian. The knighting ceremony was held in the chapel with the gold.

Being knighted was a great honor. I did not understand at the time how great an honor it was. This was the first knighting ceremony in Russia in seventy years. When the knights of Malta were defeated by Napoleon in 1798, they were disbursed. One third went to England; the monarch of England could bestow a knighthood. One third went to Rome, where the Pope could bestow a knighthood. One third went to Russia, where the czar could bestow a knighthood. But the czar was killed in 1918 when the communist party assumed control. But with the fall of the communist party that authority had been given to the Patriarch of the Russian Orthodox Church.

# MY JAMES BOND JOURNEY TO ARMENIA

In 1989 I was getting ready to go to Washington, D.C. to participate in the prayer service the night before the inauguration of President George H.W. Bush. I was requested by the Republican National Committee to come to Washington and give a prayer. A few days before I left for Washington Armenia had an earthquake. Twenty-five thousand people were killed in their homes. Many people who survived were now in the streets because their homes were gone.

When I heard the news I picked up the phone and made many phone calls to private agencies and public companies to find food, blankets, bottled water and other supplies to take there. I really wanted to help Armenia. Most people don't know but the Kingdom of Armenia was the first state in the world to adopt Christianity as its religion. They did this back in the fourth century. They were established by the Apostle Bartholomew. Even today the Armenian Apostolic Church is recognized as the oldest national church. It is still recognized as the country's primary religious establishment.

I knew these people had to get through the winter as well as the earthquake. The army agreed to loan me a C-47 to take everything to Armenia. But I couldn't get permission to fly over Russia to Yerevan, Armenia. Armenia is landlocked. The only way to get there is over Russia. This was still during the cold war. The Soviet Union dominated Armenia. Armenia didn't have an embassy in the United States so I couldn't get a visa to go to

Armenia. I couldn't get a visa to go to the Soviet Union. They had no desire to help a Christian charity. I was really running up against a stone wall. I had a C-47 full of stuff and couldn't deliver the needed supplies. No permits, no visas!

I flew to Washington for the Inauguration. I went to the Cathedral for the Protestant Prayer service. The Roman Catholics have their own service. I was waiting in the green room for us to be called to walk inside. There were a dozen or so different denominations and churches represented. I was dressing in my clerical regalia. There was a very distinguished gentleman next to me with a long beard, also dressing, who asked me who I represented. I told him and asked him the same question. He said, "I am the Catholico of the Armenian Apostolic Church."

I almost cried when he told me. I said, "I am so sorry to hear about the earthquake in your country. Sir, I have been trying for three days to find a way to bring a C-47 full of supplies to help your people. But I can't get permission to fly over Russia to deliver the food. I can't get visas to enter the country"

He looked at me and asked, "When do you want to go?"

I said, "I will leave tomorrow."

We left the green room to walk down the aisle of the cathedral. With each step he whispered instructions. We were surrounded by hundreds of people attending the Inauguration Prayer Service. With each step he whispered very specific instructions. He leaned over to me and began, "Fly to Cairo, Egypt."

"Go to the Cairo Museum."

"Go to the curio shop."

"You will meet a man named Alex."

"Alex will arrange everything."

With that we climbed the steps to the platform and had the prayer service.

After the service, we returned to the green room. As we were taking off our clerical regalia, he asked again when I would be leaving. I assured him I would leave the next day. He seemed to be satisfied with that. He again said everything would be prepared. I never spoke to that man again in my life. I called Betty and told her that I was leaving the country. I wasn't sure where I was going and didn't know when I would be back. The next morning I boarded a plane for Cairo.

I arrived in Cairo. I took a taxi immediately from the airport to the Cairo Museum. It is one of the largest in the world. It has some of the great antiquities of the ancient world. Scholars from all over the globe go there to study the culture and society of ancient Egypt. On the way I wondered how many curio shops there would be in the museum. I found the only curio shop. I was beginning to wonder how I would recognize Alex or he would recognize me. I walked toward the curio shop and there was a man standing in the door. I am still about ten feet from him when he looked straight at me and said, "You're Lonnie Rex. Don't speak English. Don't say a word."

He led me outside of the museum to a tiny car. We got into the car and he drives me out into the desert. He didn't say much, his English was very poor. He said to me, "When Russia invaded Armenia. The Armenian Apostolic Church took their artifacts which dated back to Apostle Bartholomew, and brought them to the desert of Cairo, to the catacombs. We have all of our Armenia Apostolic Church artifacts in there. We are going there, which are very secret."

He stops the car. We walk to a door. He leads me down several flights of stairs into the depths of the desert. I have never seen anything like it in my life. He led me past ossuaries where they claim contain the bones of one of the Twelve. They have other artifacts which they say are over nineteen hundred years old. Finally, he led me to a radio room. He walked over and typed on an ancient teletype machine. A few seconds later the teletype machine clattered again as a message was received.

He said, "Come with me. Here is a ticket to the Aswan Dam. This is an airline ticket that will take you to the Aswan

Dam. Once you get there, take the second ticket and get on the Sheraton Cruise Liner. It will bring you down the Nile. It will take seven days to do this. It will go down the river at night and stop in the day time so you can visit various tourist destinations such as the pyramids, the Valley of the Kings, King Tut's Tomb, and many others. It is the history of civilization. When you get back to Cairo, I will have all of the arrangements made."

He drove me to a tiny airport. I got on the plane to the Aswan Dam. When I got off the plane I took a cab to the Sheraton Cruise Liner where I had a lovely room about five feet wide. We floated down the Nile River. It was one of the greatest experiences of my life. We would float down the Nile at night. In the day time we would leave the ship and visit some of the greatest archeological treasures in the world. Every day the process was repeated again with different treasures to look at the next day. At night I was able to check in with my office in Tulsa.

When I got to the end of my journey down the Nile and arrived back in Cairo, Alex met me at the boat. He reached in his pocket and handed me an airline ticket. He said, "This is your ticket to Paris. Once you are in Paris, go to the Armenian Embassy, the Ambassador will have instructions for you from there." I was sure there would be a ticket to Russia this time. He told me, "Here is the address and the directions to the Armenian Embassy." He also handed me some French Francs for the taxi.

I flew to Paris. I grabbed an airport taxi and went to the Armenian embassy. I walked up to the desk and a lady looks up and says, "You're Lonnie Rex." I nodded my head.

The Armenian Ambassador comes out of his office. He tells me to follow him. He personally drove me to the airport. That surprised me. He handed me a ticket and said, "Here is your ticket to Moscow. Here is your visa. When you get there go to the Armenian Embassy. The Ambassador will have instructions for you." He also handed me some Russian rubles for the taxi.

The American Presidential Inauguration is on January 20. By now it is near the first of February. I am flying to Moscow in the middle of the winter without a heavy winter coat. All I have with me is an overnight bag. I thought I would be in Washington one night and then back to Tulsa. Now I am traveling with a suit and another change of clothes and a shaving kit.

I landed in frigid Moscow. I take an airport taxi to the Armenian embassy. I walk up to the lady at the desk. She looks at me and says, "You're Lonnie Rex. We've been expecting you. One moment the ambassador will be with you." I nodded my head.

He walks out of his office. He led me down a hallway to a back entrance. We go outside and get into a car which takes me to a little private airport outside of town. He puts me on a very small plane. It probably only had seats for a dozen people or so. I was the only passenger on the plane. The Ambassador tells me, "You are going to Yerevan, Armenia."

I was glad to finally being going to Armenia. I was a little bothered by the small plane. It took several hours to travel the thousand miles from Moscow to Armenia. I land in Armenia in the evening. I was beginning to feel real grimy. I hadn't changed clothes since I left Cairo. It was also bitterly cold. I climbed out of the small plane and walked into a very small airport. It was about the size of a nice American home. All of the walls in the airport were glass. We were well outside of the world of custom agents and passports. I am standing in the airport all alone. I think to myself, "Well, I am in Armenia. Surely somebody is expecting me."

About that time a man walks up to me. He was to be my driver for the entire time I was in Armenia. About the same time I look out upon the airport runway and I see a C-47 beginning to land. It pulled around the airport gate. Two Americans jump out, ready to unload the food and supplies.

I was in Armenia for nearly two weeks. I supervised the distribution. The Armenian Church put me up in the best hotels they had available. I ate the finest Armenian cuisine there was.

They provided the driver, truck, interpreter and helpers. They took care of all of my expenses for the entire ten days. They also shared some details about the history of their great church. They showed me some of the apostles' artifacts which had been returned to their country from the Soviet Union. They have a special chair in the throne room for the Catholicos of their church. He sits in the chair when his promotion is announced. They honored me by allowing me to sit in the chair. They took pictures of me there. I really treasure those pictures.

When the job was over I took a flight to Moscow. From there I took a direct flight back to the United States on a commercial plane. I left nearly a month earlier for a three day stay in Washington to attend a presidential prayer service.

I use this in speeches as an example of God's timing. God does lead us. God does guide us. God does go before us. God does give us the words to say. God does speak if we are willing to listen. Sometimes He has to hit me over the head with a 2 X 4. But I try to be more sensitive to the voice of God. I try to listen to that voice inside of me. I love to tell these stories because it shows that if God was with me then, He is with me now. These are not stories they are testimonies.

That's why I like my GPS in the car. If that lady can find me in the car and knows where I am, and can tell me when to turn right and when to turn left. Then God knows where I am. He can tell me when I make a wrong turn and tell me to make a legal U-turn.

God truly does work in mysterious ways. The Catholico of the Armenian Church was actually in New York for a business meeting. He was invited to the prayer service at the last second. Then he was randomly chosen to walk down the aisle beside me. In the life of a Christian, there are no accidents, only Divine appointments.

# THE INCREDIBLE JOURNEY TO NORTH KOREA

The Ambassador from North Korea to Russia watched the telethon I appeared on with Gorbachev. We were raising money for the children of Afghan veterans. He wrote down my name. North Korea was still mourning the loss of their "Great Leader", Kim Il-sung had died. He had been succeeded by his son, Kim Jong-il. They were having a real famine.

I get a call at five o'clock one morning. I picked up the phone beside my bed wondering if some of my family had an emergency. Nothing showed on the caller ID. I have an unlisted telephone number. The voice on the other end of the line said, "This is the government of Democratic People's Republic of Korea calling, would you come to North Korea?"

I said, "Yes, when would you want me to come?"

The voice said, "Can you come today?"

I told him, "I will leave today, but I will have to fly to Los Angeles. Then I will have to fly to Seoul, Korea, because I don't have a visa to go to China." I knew I would have to go to Beijing to fly to North Korea. Then I continued, "We have an office in Seoul."

The voice interrupted me, "Yes we know."

I continued, "I will spend a couple of days there getting a visa to China. Then I will fly to Beijing. I will go to your embassy there and get a visa to travel to North Korea"

It took me four days to get to China. I no more got off the plane in Beijing than I was met by seven North Korean agents. I hadn't told anyone what plane I would be on but they knew. That was kind of eerie. They took me to the Traders hotel. They told me to give them my passport for a visa. They were leaving and would be gone a couple of hours. I should lock the door. I should not answer the phone. No one should be allowed to come in. I had to trust them because they had my passport but it was spooky. In a couple of hours they came back.

They said they would be back in the morning. I was to stay in the room. Food would be delivered at seven o'clock. I was not to open the door but wait until they left to pick up the tray. The next morning they came back. We went to the airport. Two of them accompanied me onto the plane. It was an old Russian built small passenger plane with canvas seats. I really wondered if it would get off the ground. There were two flights a week into North Korea, Tuesday and Friday. These were the only flights into North Korea from the outside world.

North Korean Visa

I landed in North Korea. I was met by an interpreter. He took me into the airport and took my passport. We got into a small Mercedes. I thought we would go to a hotel. But I was put on the grounds of the Great Leader in a guest house. I was the only guest but there were three workers in the house to see to all of my needs. They took care of my food, my laundry, my bed, I was treated like royalty.

That night, seven North Korean top officials came to meet with me. They started reading from a scroll, telling me this was what they wanted me to give them. They started out with things like four hundred metric tons of rice, two hundred metric tons of paper to print children's school books, and so on down the line. What they asked me for, a small NGO, it would have taken a half a dozen Nations to provide.

It made me mad!

A righteous indignation came upon me.

I stood up and said, "Why don't you people get smart like the Chinese? Let me bring President Carter, he has been here before. His nephew works at CNN. Let's have the great hall like the Chinese did with President Nixon. They opened China to the world. See what great things have happened for them. *Let's do that*! If you do that I will arrange for all of your list."

They all jumped up at once, and said, "Can we leave?"

I said, "Yes, you can leave."

They left. I changed clothes and went to bed. I had traveled a long ways through several time zones and I was tired. About ten o'clock the telephone rang. The voice on the other end said, "Can we come back?"

I got out of bed, put my clothes on and was waiting for them. I didn't know they had been over to talk to the Dear Leader. This time they brought another interpreter with them. He was the head of the English department for Pyongyang University. So now I had an interpreter sitting on each side. They said, "We don't believe that our interpreter understood what you said. So we want you to say again so both interpreters can agree on what you recommend."

This time I waxed eloquently. I talked and talked with both hands waving. They interpreted and interpreted. All of this time I was talking they sat very formally right in front of me. When I was finished one of the seven said to me, "Dr. Rex, you know, we have your passport. We have called your wife. We told her that you would be delayed."

That almost made me wet my pants, but I stayed calm. "That's wonderful. How can I be of service to you, if I am delayed?"

They responded, "Our dear leader wants you to speak to all of our departments. We have never had anyone to speak to us like you have spoken to us."

The next day, every move I made was recorded by a television camera. Every night, everything I did that day was broadcast on North Korean television. Of course the South Koreans were able to pick up that signal. In turn, it was sent to the American embassy. The White House knew where I was, and what I was doing the entire time I was there. I called the White House before I left to let them know I had been invited to North Korea.

The first night, they took me to the circus. They took me to the area where the circus people lived and trained together. I was then taken into a 10,000 seat arena. The only people in the entire arena consisted of my interpreters and I. They presented a complete circus like the place was full to overflowing.

The next day, I was taken to a hospital. I walked in the hospital and found naked people on gurneys. I finally realized they had leeches all over them, sucking out poison. They had no Western medicine. They had no antibiotics. In another ward people were being treated with acupuncture. I watched an operation with acupuncture used as anesthetic. I must say, it did work.

The next day, we went to the opera. North Koreans love the Opera. It was a huge Opera House. There was a complete program presented with sets, make-up and costumes. Again we were the only people in the audience.

The next day we went to a special Children's Building. It was a beautiful ten story building in downtown Pyongyang. If children take music lessons of any kind they take the lessons in the children's building. I played the piano for them. I went from room to room, talking with them and answering questions from the children as well as the adults. I was the first American they had ever seen. At the end of the day they presented a one hour musical program just for me. They had outstanding talent.

In my mansion, I knew my room was bugged but one morning I found proof. I woke up early and the sun was hitting the wall in front of my bed. When I looked at the wall I saw something out of ordinary. I glanced back at the wall and saw a tiny camera. The light had captured the small lens of the camera. I got up, turned my back to the camera, got dressed and walked toward the bathroom. I'm not sure why I turned my back to the camera. I had already been there a few days. It wasn't like there was something new to see. I washed my face and shaved. Out of the corner of my eye I saw another camera in the bathroom! I got in the shower. By this time I am a little paranoid. At the top of the shower there was another camera!

I was supposed to stay from Tuesday until Friday, but instead I stayed from Tuesday until the following Tuesday. I had a ball. They treated me like a Head of State. The interpreters and I bonded that week. They were by my side the entire week. They would pick me up in the morning and drop me off in the evening. I thought they were considering my recommendation of becoming more open. They would ask me questions. Did I really think that CNN would bring their cameras in and televise their country? Did I really know President Carter's nephew who worked at CNN? On the eighth day after I arrived I left. I had to retrace my steps to come home; North Korea to Beijing, Beijing to Seoul, Seoul to Los Angeles, and Los Angeles to Tulsa.

The morning after I got home. my phone rang at five o'clock again. This time it was one of my interpreters from North Korea.

He was all happy asking how I was and so forth. He told me that he was glad I got home safely and then he asked the magic question, "Can you come back"?

I said, "Sure, when did you want me to come back?"

He responded, "Today."

I always let the White House know what was going on. I knew that going to North Korea is not something Americans do every day. I got a telephone call from my senator, Senator Jim Inhofe. He told me, "Lonnie, you can't go back over there. We have no government representatives there and if you get in trouble there is nothing we could do."

I said, "Senator, I am not going as a representative of the United States government. I am going as the leader of Non-Government Organization. I am going as a Humanitarian. I go anywhere, anytime, I am invited. I go where there is a need."

When I got back the second time I called him and gave him a report. He had seen the reports of where I had been because the North Koreans had televised everything on their state television. Senator Inhofe asked me when I was going back. He wanted to go with me the next time I went. He never went with me to North Korea.

When they called for the second visit, I reminded them I would have to travel from Tulsa to Los Angeles, from Los Angeles to Seoul, from Seoul to Beijing and then finally to North Korea. They understood so I got everything packed and traveled back to North Korea for my second adventure there. This was the trip where I learned how I got invited to go to North Korea. The North Korean Ambassador to Russia had seen me on television with Gorbachev. He reported this to his superiors. They decided that if I could work with Gorbachev, I would be acceptable to work with them. On my second visit Ambassador Rhee met me in Beijing. He had a second home in Beijing. I went to his home and had dinner with him and his family. That was when he told me.

The second time I visited North Korea, I stayed in the Kumsusan Memorial Palace where their first president, Kim Il-sung's body is preserved upstairs in a glass coffin. It was a huge mansion so I didn't care. I was met by my two interpreters. Since the first visit when they didn't believe the first one interpreted accurately, I always had the two. I really learned to love those guys.

This time they drove me a hundred miles from the capital in an old Mercedes. I wasn't sure what they were going to do with me. As we were driving down the highway they turned to me and said they would like to ask me some questions to help pass the time on our journey. They got out their pads and pencils and the interpreter who was the university professor of English said to me, "We watch American television. We hear a lot of English words we don't know the definition of. We would like to know the definition of these words we don't know. I teach in the university so I want to know."

I told them, "Fine, I don't mind. What's the first word?"

He said, "What does the word —— mean?" He asked about a very vulgar word which is unfortunately used in cable television.

I thought, "Oh, my God." But I tried to answer the question as honestly as I could under the circumstances. He proceeded to give me a list of words that often were vulgar and obscene. This was not one of America's finest hours. But these men were sincere in trying to understand the American language and culture. I did try to explain that to some parts of American culture these words were offensive and upsetting. But I also had to admit that to other Americans these words were totally acceptable. One of the problems was the change of the meaning of words over time. For example, when I was young a gay person was a happy person. Today a gay person is a male homosexual. There were many words that had changed their meaning over time. They were taught English from a 19th century British tradition.

In some ways, I was stunned but in another way I was pleased. These questions demonstrated how comfortable the interpreters were with me that they felt they could ask these questions.

The conversation ended as we reached our destination. We arrived in a mountain. Going there was the highest honor they could bestow upon me. We went inside the mountain. Many years ago they had dug inside this mountain. They wanted to protect treasures from potential bombs. They built huge rooms, elaborately decorated, with glass walls. Each room represented the gifts given to their Dear Leader by one country. There were rooms for Russia, various African countries, the Philippines, China, and other countries. For instance in the Russian room, they had a locomotive. There was also a limousine. They had many smaller gifts as well. The other countries had given similar gifts. They took me from room to room showing me the gifts. This represented the last fifty years of gifts.

Finally I realized what was missing. I asked them, "Where is the room with the gifts from the United States of America"? They led me to a small room, about the size of a typical bedroom in an American home. There were three gifts in there. They were under glass cases. One gift was a large ceramic eagle Billy Graham had given them when he conducted a crusade there. President Jimmy Carter has presented them with a large silver engraved cup. So I asked them, "Where are you going to put my gift"?

They said "We will reserve a place for you in here."

After we left the mountain they took me to the Demilitarized Zone or DMZ area which separates North and South Korea. I went in the building where the Armistice was signed declaring a truce and ending the Korean Conflict. Many people are able to see North Korea from the south side of the zone but not many people are able to see it from the North side. I was the only American to have that honor up to that point. I was very privileged. While I was there the North Korean government appointed me to the Peace Committee of North and South Korea.

Every time I went to North Korea they took me to the Artist colony. This is where they take their top artists who live and create together. I have eleven paintings from some of their top artists.

Their ambassador had them shipped straight to me through Beijing. After a few days I went back home.

About a month later I received another call. An American by the name of Evan Hunziker, had been arrested as a spy. He swam across the Yalu River, also called the Amrok, from China into North Korea. He was drunk and naked. When he got to the other side, a Korean farmer noticed a tall naked American. He called the officials and the man was immediately arrested. He announced that he had come to bring revival to North Korea. Of course, they called him a spy. They placed him in prison as a spy. This resulted in horrible worldwide press. This is what prompted the call from North Korea. It was the voice of my interpreter, "Lonnie, will you come back to North Korea? Have you heard about the American spy?"

I told him I heard about the spy. I told him I had read about him in the newspaper. He then shocked me when he said, "Lonnie, if you will come to North Korea, we will give you the d—— American spy."

I said, "I will be on my way today."

When I landed in North Korea, I noticed a plane from the United Nations on the tarmac. I asked about it. They said, "That is a plane the American UN Ambassador Bill Richardson came in. He wants the spy. Bill Clinton doesn't want anyone else to get credit for picking up the spy."

I knew Bill Richardson well. When I was on the board of the Armand Hammer World College in Montezuma, New Mexico, Bill was the United States representative from New Mexico. He attended several of our graduations.

They took me back to the palace. I was upset. I had spent a lot of money to get there. I had money with me to help obtain the release of the American. I wanted the credit for my NGO. I knew the publicity would go all over the world. I thought I would take us to another level. They had *called me* and told me that if I came I could have the prisoner.

Here I am in the palace guest house. This time only three men came to visit me. They said, "You know Bill Richardson is here. He came to get the release of the prisoner. They heard you were coming and they didn't want you to get the credit.'

I told them, "I know Bill Richardson."

They went on to announce to me, "We have demanded $50,000 ransom. But Bill Richardson will not give it to us!"

I looked at them and said, "Now boys, let me tell you something. I don't represent the United States. I represent Lonnie Rex, no one else. Only my thoughts, and I don't know the rules and policies of the United States government, and I don't want to know. I will tell you what I think. You called me because you like what I think and what I say." They nodded their heads; all five of them, the three government officials and the two interpreters. "The American government will not pay ransom. They can't. By their laws they can't. But let me tell you something, this boy is not a spy."

They said, "Do you know him?"

I replied, "No, but America does not have dumb spies. Anybody who says they swam across the river to convert the North Koreans to Christianity is dumb! He is not an American spy!" They laughed and laughed, they thought what I said was funny.

I continued with them, "Let me ask you a question. You have had this man for two or three months. You have had expenses to bring him from the China border to here."

"You had to keep him in the jail."

"You had to feed him."

"You had many other expenses, right?"

"Didn't you have about $50,000 worth of expenses taking care of him?"

They immediately agreed, "Yeah, Yeah, we had about $50,000 in expenses."

I said, "You go tell Bill Richardson that you had $50,000 expenses taking care of this dumb American. You be sure you call him dumb. Don't call him a spy."

They left. They did what I told them to do. But it wasn't long before they were back. They yelled at me, "*We got the money!*"

Then they said to me, "We have a problem. Bill Richardson wants to take this man home on the United Nations plane. But we promised you. Now we are men of integrity. We promised you and we will stand by our word."

I told them, "I came prepared to take him home. I have money in my briefcase to buy the airline ticket for him to go to Beijing, and then to Seoul and then to Seattle where he lives. I came prepared to do what you ask me to do. I am a man of my word. I am a man of integrity. I will do what I said I would do."

They were puzzled, "What should we do?"

I knew the answer, "Let me ask you a question. You are responsible to do what is the best for your country? What is best for North Korea? That's what you have to think. You represent the people of North Korea'. They each sat there very quietly. No one moved or made a sound.

"If I take the boy and we have to land in Beijing. With all of the publicity, think what the press will do when we land? They will know I have the famous American spy. Then we have to fly to Seoul, South Korea, your archenemy. Think what the press will do when I land there with the famous American spy. They will go wild. Then think what they will do when I land in Seattle with the famous American spy. It will be all over CNN and all over all of the other media. But if you give him to Bill, he can be gone in an hour and be in Seattle before anyone knows it. Now think, what is best for North Korea?"

They said, "Will you be mad"?

I told them, "I have to think what will be best for the government, not what will be best for me."

They were amazed with this. I could see their astonishment in their faces. I knew what was about to happen so I pushed them a little. "You better go down and tell them so they can be ready to go." They jumped up and ran out of the room. They hardly said anything at all.

In a few minutes they were back. They simply said, "Boy gone."

I asked them, "What are we going to do now?"

"Let's go play," they replied.

They entertained me royally for a few days. I had a great time while I was there. This would be the last time I was in North Korea. When I got on the plane my interpreter gave me a DVD of my first visit. He had narrated the entire DVD into English for my benefit. It covered all of the activities I had participated in during my first visit. When I got back to my office in Tulsa I received a visit from the CIA. I expected that because they had come to the office before after every visit to North Korea.

After my visits to North Korea I was able to bring eight North Korean officials to the Carter Center in Atlanta for a peace conference. Arrangements were made through the UN for them to go to Washington, D.C. But since there are no diplomatic relations between the United States and North Korea they were not able to meet with President Clinton. But they did meet with several senators who arranged for several shipments of rice to be sent to North Korea because of the famine. Through the Carter Center we were able to work with Coca-Cola to make the arrangements for several North Korean athletes to come to the 1996 Olympics in Atlanta. Coca-Cola sponsored them and paid all of their expenses. They also brought their security and cooks. They rented a house for their athletes because the North Korea government did not want them to live in the Olympic Village. They were afraid of defections.

# THE MINISTRY IN SOUTH KOREA

I know your enthusiasm and sincerity for helping us. I learned many things from you. So, I could construct the children's dormitory in 1984. May God's wonderful blessings be with you always.

—Jung, Hee Young Directress of Orphanage
Home #27 South Korea

Not long after the NGO had first opened, I was visiting in Seoul, South Korea. This was not long after the end of the Korean Conflict. The airport in Seoul must be twenty miles from the heart of the city. That first time I went to Seoul, I must have only seen three cars all the way into town. Everyone else was walking, riding a bicycle, or using public transportation. Today it is a total traffic jam.

We had opened the first few orphanages. I met the trainer for the Olympic South Korean boxing team. He had a nice training facility. He came to me and said, "I have a real problem. Kids love to come and watch me train the boxers. Most of these boys are homeless and hungry. I take them home and my wife feeds them. But my wife is giving me fits. I've got to get some help. Will you help me build an orphanage for them? I will run it if you will help me build it."

I tried to explain to him, "I don't have the money today but I will tell you what I do have. I have a new machine from South America. If your boys will get dirt, put it in there with a cup of water and a cup of cement, it will make one building block at a time. There is a long handle about ten feet long. Get three or four of these boys to jump up and down on the handle and apply pressure. This will compact that dirt. Then sit the block out in the sun for seven days and it makes a strong building block."

He agreed to try.

I came back in about three months. They had enough building blocks for us to build a building. The building would take care of the needs of twelve boys. After a few months I went back to South Korea again. They said, "Lonnie, we have never stopped making blocks. We have twelve more boys." They had enough blocks for us to build another building.

They never stopped building blocks. We didn't stop building buildings until we built a village. The government gave us land on the side of a mountain to build the village. Eventually there were enough buildings to house two thousand boys, a trade school for two thousand boys to learn a trade, and a church that seats 2,500.

*All built by one machine making one block at a time!*

I never started out to build something great. I assumed one building for twelve boys would satisfy the need. But the boys continued to build blocks. From the trade school they made all of the doors, laid the tile, made the furniture, sewed the draperies, and sewed all of the sheets and pillows. We bought nothing but the raw materials. The boys made everything we needed. It was a great joy for Betty and me to go to the Sunday church services and worship with these two thousand boys singing and praising God.

We also helped leprosy villages in South Korea. We would provide a pastor and a school. The children were not able to go to school because if they live in the village and rubbed any open sores, they will get leprosy. People don't want to send their children to school with the children of the lepers for fear they will get the disease. So the children of the lepers are forced to stay in the village. They are basically quarantined there.

The South Korean government was supporting these villages with very basic food to eat. They lived in shacks made out of cardboard and wood they found on the ground. I asked the government to give me the leprosy villages. I had a plan to make them self-supporting and the government would no longer have that obligation. That was either a dumb idea or a brilliant idea. So they agreed.

The staff asked me what I was going to do. They weren't sure if I hadn't gone off the deep end. We never had the money to do what I stepped out to do. But I would always end up telling them if they weren't happy they should go where they would be happy. When God opens the door I am going to walk through that door.

I went to the hatchery. I bought baby chicks. There were ninety families living in this village in the mountains outside of Seoul. We gave each leper family three hundred baby chicks. I gave them enough polyethylene to build a chicken house. We gave them enough chicken feed to raise them to brooder size. Then we threatened them within an ounce of their life if they ate a chicken.

The next time I visited the village there were chickens everywhere. With each of the ninety families starting with three hundred chicks, there were thousands of chickens. When I drove up to the village there was a motorcycle with crates of chickens tied to the back. I don't know how he balanced so many chickens on the cycle. But he was taking chickens to market. They became self-supporting. Soon each family was making enough money to build a nice little hut. We built them a church and sponsored the pastor for a year. We built a school and sponsored the teacher for a year.

After we helped this village, we went to the next leper village. This one was smaller with only forty or so families. The terrain was different around this village. We gave each of the families a pregnant sow. We also gave the village one boar. In a short period of time there were piglets everywhere. They soon were self-supporting as well. The next village we gave chickens again. The fourth village got pregnant cows and a bull. That village had more pasture land. The final village we helped got pigs. Within a year, all six of the leper villages were self-supporting. Each had a church and pastor as well as school with a teacher.

As the villages were becoming self-supporting, they began to become more ambitious. The first village came to me. They had no source of water in the village so they had to bring the water into the village by hand with buckets. They found out it would take ten thousand dollars to bring the water from the spring to the village. This would place several facets in the middle of the compound. But I was teaching them business. I didn't give them ten thousand dollars. But I did loan them ten thousand dollars. The second village heard about the first one getting water so they wanted water too. When the first village paid off their loan, I moved the money to the second village. That same ten thousand dollars put water in all six villages.

By the time the last village had water, the first village now wanted electricity. Each hut would have one light bulb. So now the ten thousand dollars made a second round through all of the villages giving them electricity.

We had the largest deaf and mute orphanage in South Korea. Betty and I enjoyed so much going there. The love of those kids for us was very inspiring. I loved their little orchestra. Each of our homes in South Korea had a plot of ground and raised most of their food. Each of the children had their chores. Each fall we had a big festival with each home making kimchee, their staple for the winter. Kimchee is a Korean traditional fermented dish of vegetables with seasonings. They make it in huge pots that go in the ground and are stored there for the winter.

We had a large baby intake home. There would often be twenty to twenty five babies in cribs. We had from one to three babies left on our doorstep several nights a week. They had been produced by the American soldiers and their Korean girlfriends.

From our homes we delivered ten adopted babies to Los Angeles. Every Wednesday delivered ten babies to Chicago.

Every Friday we deliver ten babies to New York. Many volunteers in Korea and the United States made this possible. We had an adoption agency in Tulsa that took care of the American paperwork. Our office in Seoul took care of the Korean paperwork.

One year I had the biggest surprise for my birthday. A noted businessman who loved our work in South Korea bought round trip airline tickets from Seoul to Tulsa for twelve of our orphanage directors and staff. They came to help celebrate my birthday. It was a great surprise! It was a great gesture because none of the twelve had ever been to America. I knew nothing until I walked in our chapel and the Koreans started shouting Happy Birthday! Royce had arranged for all of their housing and entertainment.

He had been to South Korea several times so he knew that steak was very, very expensive there. If you ordered steak it was typically the size of an Eisenhower silver dollar. He took them to Jamil's, one of the best steak houses in Oklahoma. He arranged with Mr. Jamil to provide each of them with a twenty-four ounce T-bone steak which covered a platter. You never heard such *oohs* and *aahs*. They devoured the steaks down to the bone and cleaned the bone Korean style.

He also impressed them when he took them to our home. In Korea ice cream is a luxury. It came in small dips at a high price. We arranged for big bowls of a pint or larger of ice cream for everyone. For years, each time I went to South Korea they would talk about the T-bone steaks and ice cream.

In time the president of South Korea honored me with a Presidential Humanitarian Award. They wanted to honor me for taking six villages of lepers, off of the government dole and not only self-supporting but flourishing. All of these ideas came to me from God. I don't pray for money, I pray for ideas. God gives the ideas, it is his responsibility to see that I have the money to carry them out.

# ETHIOPIA — WHERE THE BABIES ARE SILENT

The trip I took with you in March of 1985 to Nairobi, Kenya and Ethiopia, was one of the benchmarks of your ministry. The joy you brought to a dying Ethiopian on his cot at the Refugee Camp, was something I shall always remember with gratitude.

—Philip D. Egert

Emperor Haile Selassie had been the leader of Ethiopia for many years. But in 1974, the Communist got rid of him and created a Communist government. The Communists led by the Russians took fifty of the top leaders of the country into the square in the capital and shot them all. One of those shot was the treasurer of the country.

I had the privilege of staying in the mansion of his widow. She gave us a great history of the country telling us how great it was and how rich it was. She told us that she and her husband had mansions in several parts of the country. When the communists took over the country they left her with her primary residence in the capital city, Addis Ababa. We were guests there.

The home was very beautiful with very nice furnishings. There was an elaborate dining table with place settings at every chair, but there was no food on the table. There were these young girls who surrounded the table, one behind every person. They each had a little plate of food. There were plate settings but no utensils. I looked around for chop sticks, forks, spoons, knives or something. I didn't know what we were going to eat with but I

159

was too embarrassed to ask. But then I found out how we were going to eat. The little girls hand fed us from the small plate they were holding. When I started to get my fill I motioned to them that I was full. But they would motion back to me, one more handful, one more. They stuffed us full and I loved every minute of it. When I returned home, Betty wouldn't feed me like that.

The reason I came to Ethiopia was because the Canadian government had given us a large shipment of dried milk for the Ethiopian families. When the Communists took over they drove the Christians up to the desert on the border of Kenya. They knew they had to destroy the Christians in order to have complete control of the country. There were over a million people in tents waiting to die when the BBC press discovered them.

When I arrived in Ethiopia I wanted to meet the Patriarch of the Coptic Church to assist in customs free importing of the goods for the famine area. This church is the oldest continual Christian Church in the world, even pre-dating the Roman Catholic Church. Their church dates to the time of the Apostles. Their church was founded by the Ethiopian Eunuch who was baptized by Philip the Evangelist, one of the original deacons in the Jerusalem Church. They claim to have the bones of an Apostle in their artifacts in their catacombs.

I was able to meet with the Patriarch a couple of times. He was gracious and took his picture with me. The President of the Lions Club was a Coptic Christian. The Lions Club would transport us to the famine camps in their private plane. They would fly us to the area where the Communists had driven the Christians.

We flew to the camp where the Christians were huddled together in tents or worse. They said there were a million of them. When we landed there were tents as far as you could see. I was amazed that on the top of every tent was a Coptic Cross. I didn't know what a Coptic Cross was. It is shaped differently than a traditional western cross. The pilot of the plane was a Coptic Christian so he explained the cross to me. He told me these were all Christians, driven up here to die.

160

While I was there I made arrangements for our supplies to get there. We had a shipload of food, blankets, and other supplies coming. The supplies did get there through arrangements made with the Lions Club and the Coptic Church. The meeting with the Patriarch of the Ethiopian Coptic Church laid the groundwork for that to happen.

Lonnie and the patriarch of the Ethiopian orthodox church

While I was there the Red Cross gave me a tour of some of the tents. In one tent there were ninety bodies lying on grass mats on the ground, wrapped up in saris. I thought this was their morgue. It was as silent as a morgue. I asked if this was the morgue, their response was stunning. They said, "No, these are the women who have had babies in the last two or three days." He led me down an aisle, he would speak to them and they would unwrap their garments and speak to him. They would show they had no milk in their breast to feed their babies. My heart began to weep. As

161

we walked down the aisle the women would open their garments and show their newborns. He said to me, "These are ninety babies three days old or less."

I said to him, "I just had a new grandson. I was in the hospital nursery with ten or twelve babies and they were all screaming, it was a noisy place. Here I thought I was in the morgue"!

He said, "Dr. Rex, these babies don't have the strength to cry."

That was the day I made up my mind, I am the voice of those who don't have the strength to cry. That phrase is on every Who's Who I have ever filled out in the world. I want everyone to know I am the voice of those who don't have the strength to cry.

When I got back to the states, the story of the camps and the famine in Ethiopia had hit the newspapers in London and around the world. We got together two or three containers of food, clothing and blankets for the camps. It was going to take $105,000 to ship those containers to Ethiopia. I didn't have $105,000. I got an idea and when I get an idea I think it is from the Lord. Rev. Marvin Gorman was a good friend and I had worked with his sons on our television station for our telethons. He had bought the big First Baptist Church of New Orleans and he was packing them in. He was having five services a weekend. The Lord placed on my heart to call Marvin Gorman. I called him, "Marvin, you always like Betty's and mine twin piano concerts. Betty and I are willing to come down if you will get two pianos. We will give a piano concert if you will help us raise the $105,000 we need to send that food to Ethiopia."

He said, "Lonnie, we are building a new church. We have a great missionary program. He made every excuse in the world." I hung up.

I was so distraught I went home. I thought I had heard from the Lord. I thought the Lord was leading and guiding me. It so embarrassed me that he would turn me down. I thought the Lord had impressed me to call him. I thought this was the answer to our problem. I began to question my own spirituality. I really beat myself over the head. Why did I call? How stupid can you get?

Lord you told me to stay out of the churches. I will never go in another church. I was mad at myself. I was mad at the Church. I was about half mad at God.

The next morning, the office opened at eight and I usually got there a little before eight, when I walked in my secretary said, "Marvin Gorman has been holding on the line for fifteen minutes. I told him you would call him back but he said he would rather hold until you walked in."

I go in my office and picked up the phone and Marvin Gorman is bawling his eyes out. I thought someone had died! I yelled at him, "Marvin, what's wrong, what's wrong!" He was sobbing.

Finally he calm down and says, "Can you come Sunday?"

I said "Yes."

He responded, "Well, please come. Sunday we will have the pianos on the stage and you can take the missionary offering."

I said, "What changed your mind?"

He told me, "Lonnie, last night the Lord woke me up in the middle of the night. He told me to get up and read Matthew. I got out of bed, turned the light on. My wife said what are you doing? I told her God told me to get up and read this Scripture. She said, read it out loud, I want to hear it. He said, the Scripture says, If you do not hear the cry of the poor, I will not hear you in your time of need. Will you get down here Sunday?"

We went down on Saturday. The first service the next morning was at seven o'clock in the morning. There were five services in all ending with a five o'clock service that evening. By the third service we had raised the $105,000. Marvin came over to me. He said, "Lonnie, can I go with you?"

I said, "Sure." In the fourth and fifth services I raised enough money to take him, his son, and his film crew with me. It really touched him. When he came back he went on television and raised a million dollars for his new building.

Later he said to me, "See what I would have missed if God hadn't put me right."

My last trip to Ethiopia I flew to Kenya and then took a small prop plane to Addis Ababa. It is just a short distance. When we get to the small airport, we jumped out and walked into the tiny terminal. They told me my luggage was outside to go claim it. I walked outside and saw several suitcases but mine was not there. As I am looking in the luggage area, I saw the plane take off! My heart sank. I had no idea what I was going to do! I went inside the little terminal. They said this was Tuesday and the plane would return on Friday. They would get my luggage then.

For whatever reason, there is a nice Sheridan Hotel in Addis Ababa. I had a reservation there. It was a first class hotel in the middle of this vast poverty. I got my room but I had no tooth brush, no shaving cream or razor, or anything else. I don't see how I can conduct my business looking this way. I was to meet with the head of the Lions Club, the Patriarch of the Coptic Church. I wanted to look like I should. I thought maybe I could find some things in the market.

The next morning I went down to the hotel restaurant for breakfast. I was across the dining room, next to the windows that overlooked the swimming pool. This was totally on the other side from the entrance door. Out of the corner of my eye I saw the doors open. This young girl came through and I could tell she was dragging something heavy. She was leaning with the weight. I watched her for a moment. It looked like she had a suitcase in her hand. I looked back down to my plate and continued eating. I looked back up and saw her walking towards me. But I continued eating. All of the sudden I looked down and there was my huge suitcase sitting beside me. This young girl had dragged it across the restaurant. She never said a word to anyone. She never said a word to me. She never asked my name. She sat my suitcase down and disappeared. To this day I say it was an angel. They told me the plane would not be back until Friday. I have always thanked God for my angel.

# TOUCHING LIVES IN GHANA

We decided to establish a base for humanitarian work in Ghana. I had appointed a Mr. Larsen-Perry as the director of our work there. He had formerly worked for the Ministry of Health and Social Welfare. To work in the country we had to be registered with that branch of the government. With his expertise it still took us five months to get registered. But this was absolutely necessary for the work.

After we were registered I went to Accra, Ghana, to personally oversee the work. My cameraman, Mike Tongues, had met me in Europe so we could record the work to share with the partners of the humanitarian work. The first time to Accra was interesting from the beginning. Ghana does not have a lot of electricity. What electricity they do have they don't waste on stuff like airport runways. We landed on the dark runway. Once we landed there was no bus to take us to the terminal. I walked down the dark steps, across the runway, into a dimly lit terminal. I had heard stories about what happens in the dark in Africa. The stories were not good, especially for Americans. When I walked off the plane I was very apprehensive because I had thirteen pieces of checked baggage. I was bringing cameras, lights, tapes and other equipment with me.

It was a relief to hear someone call my name. Even though it was almost pitch dark, a voice spoke out of the darkness, "I am the Chief Protocol Officer for the airport. Welcome to Ghana."

I wasn't sure if I was being arrested or welcomed but I really had no choice but to follow him. I told Mike to stay close. As we walked into the terminal we found a large group of people. Mr. Larsen-Perry had organized a welcoming party. Most of the staff and volunteer workers were there as well as the Chief Official from the Ministry of Health and Social Welfare. Two or three other Ministries were also represented. They had a receiving line set up to receive us and make sure we were welcome. It was quite the honor for us to be welcomed in such a manner.

Our passports were taken and given to the officials. We were treated like visiting dignitaries. They didn't want us to even claim our luggage personally. They assured us it would be taken care of but Mike and I knew we had to identify everything personally because there was so much. But they marched us through immigration without asking for our passports.

When we finally found our way to baggage claim, it was like looking for something in a dark closet. There were only two small fluorescent bulbs. But we finally found everything. I was worried about finding a taxi big enough to carry everything but Mr. Larsen-Perry told me there was a twenty-four passenger bus waiting on us. The Leprosy Association, a government agency, had provided the vehicle.

We had to work to get out of the airport because there was a second receiving line created by people who had arrived too late for the first receiving line. After everything was loaded on the bus we were taken to a reception. There was media from all over the country. I introduced the staff and told everyone our purpose in coming to Ghana. The next morning we were all over the television and radio stations.

On our way to the hotel that night I was reminded we were in Africa. I found out the starter on the bus didn't work. Every time we stopped, to get going again we would get off the bus and push it until we got it going fast enough for the driver to pop the clutch and get it started. In Africa these kinds of problems are normal. When we got to the hotel I unpacked with a small oil lamp. There was no water. The water was only on for fifteen minutes a day, beginning at five o'clock in the morning. You had to get up and fill the tub if you wanted a bath. They also provided two buckets you filled so you could brush your teeth and flush the toilet.

The next morning they brought me a bucket of water since I missed the five o'clock water run. I took a bath with two glasses of water, one to lather with and one to rinse. Even though the water was cold, it felt good to be somewhat clean.

That first day I traveled by bus to the Department of Rehabilitation headquarters for the rehabilitation of the blind and crippled. We had an office in their center. I was able to meet with several of the many volunteers we had. We had shipped equipment over from the United States. To the natives it seemed like it was Christmas. They sang the praises of God with true joy. It brought tears to my eyes.

I spent days helping people in many ways. We distributed ten fifty pound bags of dried milk. Hundreds of mothers came to the village with their children to get some precious strength building powder. While we were there we heard drumbeats. From the drums we knew that royalty was coming. The village chief, along with his Council, was led by a man carrying a golden rod. The people knew, as we did also, it was exceptional for the chief to welcome anyone in this manner. We later learned this was the largest region in Ghana. This made the chief the most noted ruler. He led fifty square miles and one hundred thousand people. With television cameras running I was made an honorary chief.

There was one major incident while I was there. One rainy morning they were late coming after us. We had expected to leave about seven but it was moving towards ten. All of the sudden there were screams coming from the hallway. One of the part-time workers ran into my room weeping. He told me two of our staff members had been arrested and were being hauled off to jail. They had also confiscated the equipment.

I ran down the hall and found it full of policemen. When you are tall like I am, it's not hard to get everyone's attention. I shouted into the group of police, "Stop! Come here!"

They stopped and looked at me. One told me to come with them. But I didn't waiver, "No, you come to me. You are the one that got me up out of my sleep and caused all of this commotion. You come here to my room." They followed me back down the hall.

One of the lieutenants appeared to be doing the "bullying." I looked straight in the eyes and told him, "I have a letter from your Ambassador here and I'll show it to you. But first, I want to know who you are. You don't even have any identification on you. I don't see a badge or anything. You give me your identification before I show you my official letter from your Ambassador written to the Secretary of Foreign Affairs."

They all began to dig in their pockets for a badge. The lieutenant pulled out a card which said he was an inspector born in 1952. I was certain it didn't belong to him because he obviously wasn't that old. But I told him I would show him the letter.

The letter was in English. I didn't think he could read it but it had a very official stamp on the top. But he looked it over. He folded it carefully. The men were told to step away from the equipment. He apologized to us and walked away. It turned out that when we were filming some cars lined up at a gas station, we also filmed the police station. This had upset them.

I ended that trip by touring a leper village. There were thirty-two lepers who had lived there for over thirty-five years. They loved the Lord. They gathered together and sang songs of praise to the Lord. Some were blind and crippled but their spirits were high. They sang, *He has Never Failed Us Yet*. I wept at this manifestation of faith. They told me the government gave them a dollar a year for personal expenses. I sent someone for my briefcase. I gave each of them a pound sterling. This was more than they received from the government in a year.

Before I left the government officials gave me a banquet in my honor. The former delegate to the United Nations from Ghana was there along with the Public Relations Officer for the Department of Labor and Social Welfare. There were many other government officials there along with chiefs in native costume. The next morning I packed and left for the airport. One of the staff members was arrested again when he took a picture of the airport. He was quickly released but it just added to the situation.

When I got to the airport I was met at the front door by a large number of people. They escorted me to a VIP room where government officials were usually taken. The VIP officers took care of customs and all of the television equipment. We stayed in the lounge until everything was loaded. They escorted me to the plane. It had been an amazing trip of highs and lows.

# ARREST IN GHANA

Late in 1989 I needed to go to Ghana. We had had a presence there for a long time. The main reason I was going was to take a motorcycle to the local missionary, John Koenders. He was doing a great work taking medicine to leper colonies but he had to either walk or take a bus. Buses are not the most reliable in Africa. I was also taking a case of toothbrushes to Awijn leper colony.

I started the trip tired. The Tuesday before Thanksgiving I went to the White House to meet with President Bush and Vice-President Dan Quayle. They had invited about twenty evangelicals to talk with them about issues the country was facing. Among the other guests were Oral and Richard Roberts, Jerry Falwell, Pat Robertson, and Dr. James Kennedy. I headed back to Tulsa on Wednesday. I spent Thanksgiving with Betty and the kids and left for Africa on Friday.

By the time I got to Ghana I was exhausted. As soon as I said hello with my people I went to my room at the hotel and slept for fifteen hours straight. Then I was ready to do what I had come to do. I met with Robert Boyd, our director from Scotland, and J.E. Larsen-Parry, our director there in Ghana. They had a car and a driver so we could get to where we needed to go. We all climbed in the old Datsun station wagon. Before I got in I noticed the tires were bald. I asked the driver what a new set of tires would cost. But he didn't seem to worry about it.

171

Before we left the city we stopped by a print shop to pick up some tracts they had printed. Just as we were climbing back in the car some plain clothes cops from the Bureau of Military Intelligence surrounded the car. I tried to ask them what was wrong but they didn't seem to listen. They were screaming and yelling and pointing machine guns at us. Finally one of them told us that they had been tipped off that we were printing subversive materials urging the overthrow of the government.

We tried to protest but they confiscated the car and the tracts, threw us in the back of a truck and took us to Ghanaian BMI Federal penitentiary. We knew we weren't in America. We didn't have a hearing, a phone call or anything. They didn't even read us our rights. I don't think we really had any rights. Then we were sure we didn't have any rights when they took us to the penitentiary with real criminals!

Everybody tried to explain they had the wrong guys. I told them we had been in Ghana for a long time and had helped many people. Nothing seemed to help. They told us to strip down to our boxers so they could put us in a cell with other criminals. I knew that would not be good. A couple of white guys, one American and one European would be special targets. I knew I had to do something.

We started stripping our clothes. Then I grabbed my chest. I moaned and groaned and told them I had to have my medicine back at the hotel. I did have medicine at the hotel but I really wanted the telephone in the room. I knew I needed to get word back to the States that we had been arrested. If I didn't, we could disappear and never be heard from again. So I put on a great show for them.

The chest pains got their attention. The year before an American had been arrested. He had died while they had him. It caused an international incident. They didn't want to take a chance on attracting more publicity. They talked among themselves. Then told me they would take me back to the hotel so I could take my medicine.

I climbed into the back of a truck and we proceeded to drive over normal African roads which means bumpy. I got back to the hotel. They walked me upstairs to my room. I told them I was really feeling bad, could I lie down for a few minutes? They talked among themselves again, but decided against it. So I grabbed the drugs, we went downstairs and went back to the penitentiary.

When we got back they made everyone strip to their shorts. They put everybody in separate rooms. They shouted questions at us. I thought the questions were really absurd. But I answered every one of them. But it didn't make any difference. Finally they got tired and pushed us into a cell. I knew I had to do something so I did the heart pain thing again. They tried to ignore me but after a while they asked me if I was okay. I told them I had high blood pressure and heart problems. If I didn't go somewhere and rest, I thought I would die. The guard went back and talked with his bosses. In a few minutes he come back, gave me my clothes and took me back to the hotel.

When I got back to the hotel, I told them I needed to lie down. They came in, checked around the room. They looked under the bed and behind all the furniture. All they found was my briefcase. They told me to open it but with all the pressure I was under I couldn't remember the combination. The truth was I had a lot of cash inside. In third-world countries checks and credit cards are worthless. Cash is king. I knew if I opened the briefcase the money would be gone and they would think I was worth a lot of money for ransom.

Finally, they got tired of messing with the briefcase. They called back to their bosses to see if I could lie down. After some discussion they agreed but said I would have a guard at the door. There was loud talking between them. The guard lit up a cigarette. I told him the smoke would irritate my heart condition. We talked for a bit and he said he would go outside to smoke.

I lay on the bed for a few minutes and listened for him to come back. After a few minutes when I didn't hear him I picked up the telephone next to my bed. I was shocked! I got a dial tone. I dialed O for an operator. I asked for an International operator. When the operator came on the line I gave her the number for my office in Tulsa. The number began to ring.

Back in Tulsa it was a little after five o'clock in the afternoon. I was afraid everyone would be gone. But the Lord was with me. Connie Taylor was our vice-president. She was still at the office. When she answered the phone I told her that we had been arrested. I conveyed to her that if she didn't hear from me within twenty-four hours, she should call Doug Wead at the White House and tell him what was going on. I told her to call Royce immediately and let him know what was going on.

A few minutes later, I decided twenty-four hours was not enough. I called my daughter Debbie. I told her to call Connie and change the clock to eight hours. I told her if they didn't hear from me within eight hours to call Doug. I told her to tell Royce to call the American Embassy in Ghana in the morning at two o'clock and tell them about us.

Royce called me at the hotel. He told me that when Connie called him his first call was to the White House. He had already tried to call the Embassy in Ghana but didn't get an answer. He and Debbie met at the office at ten thirty that night to get all of the phone numbers they needed. He told me everything and told me he would call the Embassy at two.

Things were happening real fast. Every few minutes I would get up and look outside for the guard. He was sitting outside the door but every little bit he would go downstairs to smoke. After a while I didn't see him for a long time. I think he decided it was easier to stay outside than to go back and forth. Royce called me again. He said he had talked with our attorney and his advice was to get to the American Embassy as fast as I could. He thought I would be safest there. That was good advice but he wasn't the one in Africa with an armed guard with a machine gun at the door.

I went to bed with all my clothes on, with my briefcase under my head. I woke around two o'clock in the morning; I stepped outside and checked for the guard. I saw no sign of him. I didn't know if he was out smoking or had found a place to sleep. I finally decided to make a run for it. I grabbed my briefcase, stepped out and looked around again. I had a story in my head for the guard if I got caught. But I didn't know if it would work. When I didn't find the guard, I kept walking. When I approached the lobby, no one was there. I tried to look around without being noticed. It seemed to be deserted, but all of the lights were on. There was no way to get across the lobby without being noticed if the guard was close. But, I decide to make run for it.

I got out of the hotel and walked towards a dirt road. In Africa taxis are not yellow with a light on top. People just drive around looking for someone needing a ride. They charge whatever they can get. I decide to take another chance so I flagged down a car. I told him I wanted a ride to the American Embassy. He told me he knew the way. At four o'clock in the morning I arrived at the American Embassy.

The first thing I saw at the Embassy was the American flag flying outside. I really did tear up because I thought I was finally safe. The only person on duty was the Marine standing guard. He told me I could sleep on the couch until the staff go there. About seven o'clock the receptionist walked in and without introduction she said, "Lonnie Rex, are you alright? We've been expecting you!"

I knew that somewhere in the world people knew about me and were working to help. About eight the ambassador walked in. The first thing he said to me was, "You're Lonnie Rex." I nodded my head. He went on, "My phone has been ringing all night about you." He said to stay there and he would go downtown and talk with the government officials to see what could be done. I could overhear phone calls all day. The Ghana government said they were coming after me. The Embassy said I was on American soil and under the protection of the American government. I was sure glad to have the marines there. I heard the British High Commission call about Robert Byrd. He was arrested with me. No one knew anything about him.

The Ambassador came back to the embassy about three or four o'clock in the afternoon. Mr. Gonzales, the First Consulate of the United States Embassy walked into my room. He said, "I've arranged for you to have house arrest. But you must go back to the penitentiary for them to interrogate you. If you don't go back, they will be very very hard on your staff."

These were not the words I wanted to hear. But I knew I had no choice. I really hated to leave American territory. But I could not let them harm the staff no matter what. He had made them promise they would take me back to the hotel in the evenings.

When I got back to the penitentiary they tried to get my briefcase open. The guards made me bring it from the hotel room. They were sure the penitentiary guards could persuade me to open it. But my briefcase had strong locks on it. They told me to open it. I tried and I tried to open it without success. Of course the truth was, I had $10 thousand inside the briefcase! After a while they began to interrogate me again. They would ask me some of the most stupid questions. But finally they ran out of questions.

They took me back to the hotel. That was the first twenty-four hours of my incarceration. I had barely settled in the room when the phone rang. They called me from the desk to tell me I had guests. Moments later the door burst open and armed police walked in. They told me that if I walked away from the hotel again they would take me to prison. I would no longer have the luxury of the hotel. They also said they would pick me up in the morning for more interrogation. I think they were embarrassed that I was able to escape.

They were barely out the door when John Koenders walked in my room. I immediately felt better. We had sent John to school to learn how to work with people who had leprosy. He was the guy I had brought the motorcycle for. He was totally unaware of the situation. With tears in his eyes he said to me, "Does that mean I won't get my motorcycle"? I hugged him and told him that I would do my best not to leave Ghana until he got his wheels.

I had just laid down when the phone rang. I wasn't sure if I should answer it or not. But I picked it up, "Lonnie Rex, are you alright? This is the White House calling. The Chief of Staff, John Sununu, now knows about your problem and President Bush will know about it soon. Doug Wead, special liaison to the President said to tell you everything will be alright. Relax, it is in our hands." I knew that Royce and the others were doing all they could but I must say I was shocked by the phone call.

I had barely placed the phone down when it rang again. Royce was on the line telling me all he was doing to help. He started on the telephone at two o'clock in the morning and continued all day. He had talked with Christians he knew from those in high government places to Pat Robertson, Paul Crouch, TL Osborn and others. He was asking everyone to pray for my release. He had called the White House, State Department and everyone else who would listen. He called the American Embassy for three hours straight and either got a busy signal or no one answered. Finally he stepped into the shower and the phone rang. It was Doug Wead at the White House telling him that everyone knew from President Bush down. He was instructed to tell Royce that everything would be all right.

I was so touched by the phone calls. I went to sleep thinking everything would be all right in the morning. It would be over. But the next morning reality hit. A stern looking guy shook me awake. They gave me a few minutes to dress and they took me away. I was questioned all day about everything in my life. They asked questions about my family from my grandmother to my kids. They asked me about the NGO. They wanted to know how much money I made, how many employees we had, what countries were we in, and everything else they could think of. It was funny. They had paper but no pens. I took two pens from my pocket and gave the pens to my interrogators. They seemed to like that but they immediately hid the pens. Late in the day they gave me a pen and paper and told me to write a summary of all of the questions and answers of everything. When I got finished they had a photographer take my picture and they fingered printed me.

I felt terrible. I hadn't eaten all day, my back and head hurt from the chair. I was worried about Robert Boyd. His health was worse than mine. He needed his medications. When they told me I could go I wasn't sure if that meant I could leave the prison or leave the country. But they still had my passport. I stepped outside. This time there was no ride. A guard hailed me a cab. He said I could stay inside the cell until he got me a ride but I didn't want anything to do with a cell.

When I got back to my hotel the phone rang again. It was Gonzales from the American Embassy. He told me he had received several cables from Washington about me. The phone rang again, this time it was the British High Commission office. They had seen Robert Boyd. His wife was sending his medications. Robert would receive them tomorrow along with some good food. I was glad to have the support of two of the most powerful countries in the world on my side.

People were working all over the world to get me out. They were trying to find out what got us arrested in the first place. They found out that some of our staff had gone to the Post Office to mail letters to donors. In the letters there was a reference to "starving children." Someone told the authorities. They had moved in, confiscated the letters, and arrested me and the others. They arrested the printer as well. The Ghana government was demanding proof that we were a legitimate Humanitarian Organization. Everyone in the world was trying to help including our friend Pope John Paul II.

After a couple of days they allowed Robert Boyd and John Koenders to come back to the hotel. We were hoping this meant the end was close. But then two guards came and grabbed him and took him back to the prison. As they were leading him away I handed him a bottle of water. He hadn't bathed or shaved in two days. He also needed his medicine. I wanted to help him anyway I could.

Everyday brought highs and low. I heard that ten Americans had been arrested for "building a church." I later learned they were expelled from the country. I got calls from the office in Tulsa as well as friends around the world. The office was building a "credibility portfolio." They were trying to show all of the good things we had done in Africa and around the world. Amnesty International called and told me that the Ghanaians probably realized they had made a mistake but didn't know what to do about it without losing face.

Lonnie arrested in Ghana

Robert Boyd was allowed to come back to the hotel again. As soon as I heard he was in the hotel I ran down to the lobby. Robert's face looked like a day-old red-baked lobster. We went outside to talk where we could not be overheard. He told me, "I've had it. I felt I would not make it at times. I have been sleeping in a cell on the cement floor with eight others in a space about the size of a small hotel bathroom. I would lay next to a big steel door with my face as close as possible to a small crack between the door and the concrete wall so I could breathe. In the daytime I was forced to walk around in my shorts under the baking African sun."

Robert had been released into the custody of the British Consulate with the understanding that he was under house arrest. He could not leave the country. He had to return to the prison every morning at nine o'clock. The British Consulate was staying with him everywhere he went. He told me that if I hadn't called the American Embassy, it would probably been several months before Ghana acknowledged we were there.

I got word that the American media was getting involved. As soon as the office in Tulsa was convinced I wasn't going home quickly, they started putting out press releases. If the governments were having problems getting us out, maybe the press could make things work. But I was still hearing bad things. Robert Boyd told me that he had heard at the prison that the same guys who arrested them had executed seventeen men the week before without a trial. I knew people everywhere were doing their best but I wasn't sure it would be enough.

While I was under house arrest, I went through my briefcase and found a letter from Dr. Hauser of Kansas City. In the letter was the name of a lady who was a Supreme Court Justice in Ghana. He had met her in the United States. Her husband was a Baptist pastor. He asked me to give her a message. I gave her a call to see if she couldn't get me out of the mess. She invited me to dinner in her home. We had a great time together. Finally, I leveled with her. I told her everything. She said to me, "Brother Rex, I am sorry I am unable to help you. There are two levels of law in Ghana; the constitution and the president's law. He does what he wants and to hell with the rest of us."

Every night I was under house arrest the Lord was there comforting me. One night in a dream the Lord spoke to me, "Be strong and courageous, and do the work. Do not be afraid or discouraged, for the Lord God, my God is with you. He will not fail you or forsake you until all the work for the service of the Temple of the Lord is finished, 1 Chronicles 28:20. When I talked with Betty in Tulsa, I told her I wanted the whole office to read that verse every day and stand with me. I told her I wouldn't read any other Scripture while I was there. That gave me the peace to sleep every night.

Robert and I tried to figure the situation out. We knew the battle was more than just political it was spiritual. I was sure that Satan was trying to stop the good we were doing. I started fasting one meal a day. Soon I got confirmation this was indeed a spiritual battle. When the battle is political, you fight it with political weapons. When the battle is spiritual; you fight the battle with spiritual weapons. Every major ministry in the world was holding us up in prayer.

We knew that this time the Ghanaians had found out that we were humanitarians doing humanitarian work and nothing else. Robert and I thought the problem was the Ghanaians didn't know what to do with us. If we were released they would lose face to the world. The longer they held us the more pressure they got from the world. We thought something had to happen to break the impasse. If something didn't happen soon, the standoff could go on indefinitely.

We had another concern. Christmas was coming soon. We not only wanted to spend Christmas with our families, we were concerned about the thousands of families that we helped every Christmas. We would give people something to eat during Christmas and if things went well, a small gift to cheer up their kids.

We got more of our prayers answered. The rest of our group was released to house arrest at the hotel. Everybody looked absolutely horrible but at least they could shower and get some fresh clothes. I was starting to feel better again but then I got a phone call from Tulsa. They thought the Ghanaians were looking for something to bring charges against me. Amnesty International told me to expect to be charged with sedition.

We were down to Saturday night. They told me to expect to be charged on Monday. I wanted to go to church on Sunday. I wanted to attend services in Aburi, where our office was located. The hotel staff didn't want us to go to church because they were afraid the government police would come in and plant evidence while we were gone. I told them I didn't care. I needed to go to church. Aburi was about thirty miles away. In this part of the world this was a leisurely ninety minute drive. They had given us back the Datsun with the bald tires. I wasn't sure it was safe but we took it anyway. By the time we got to Aburi we were late for the services at the Methodist church.

The Methodist church was about forty years old with broken windows and a decaying cement floor, but it was packed with believers. After the service the pastor talked with us about the church providing a building for a clinic. This was of course assuming we would survive our incarceration. After the service we went over to the office. There was a library at the office. It was the only library in that part of the world. We took pictures in the offices to show we had a strong presence in the country. We went to lunch at an old British garden. Aburi was in the mountains so it was much cooler than the hotel. We didn't really want to go back. When we did get back to the hotel they told us the police never came by.

I was getting more worried every day. I was about to run out of medications. I had only planned to be in Ghana for a week or so. The Embassy sent a nurse but she thought it would be several weeks before medicines would arrive. The UN Security Council sent someone by who thought they could find me a few pills. I was seeing everybody. I was hearing from everybody. But there didn't seem to be an answer.

LaDonna Osborn, TL's daughter called the office. She heard that I had been killed! Back in Tulsa, they started wearing yellow ribbons to remind everyone that we were still in captivity. The days began to become routine. Each day Robert and I would talk about the situation. Each evening we would walk around the hotel grounds. If we stretched it just right it was about two miles. That helped to pass the time. We had been good friends before but now we were really close. We got a call that former President Jimmy Carter was trying to help. He was a good friend to the Ghanaian government. But no one knew if that would help or not.

We reached the point of two weeks since our arrest. Everything seemed so stalemate. It seemed to me the situation could stay just like it was indefinitely. I got word from Tulsa that the Ghanaian government had turned the situation over to a tribunal. They would decide if I was going to be charged with something or released! They had my life in their hands. But this was the same tribunal that had ordered the execution of seventeen people without a trial. Whatever their decision, there would be no appeal.

The next couple of days we were in communication with everybody. I heard from the American Embassy. Robert heard from the British High Commission. The main thing everybody talked about was should we hire a local attorney. If we needed an attorney the American Embassy was going to try to find someone who would be familiar with the tribunal. He would know the best way to proceed. When I wasn't on the phone or talking to someone in person, I walked the grounds and prayed. I not only prayed for our situation, I was praying for Robert. He had a relapse of Malaria fever. He was trying to rest as much as possible.

We got to the sixteenth day. I was beginning to feel better. I thought the tribunal would surely see the clarity of our situation.

I gave away everything I didn't need. I was just sure I was going home in a day or two. I packed my bags. The only thing I had left was two safari suits that wouldn't fit anyone else. I even gave away all of the food I had collected. The hotel made a celebration high tea with all of the friends I had made in the hotel. I was feeling very good.

The Supreme Court Justice invited Robert and me to dinner again. Everyone was in a good mood. We had a great time talking about our faith. The Justice had a long family history of Christian pastors dating back nearly a century. We went back to the room and slept soundly. We were absolutely certain we would be going home soon. We expected good news by ten o'clock the next morning.

Robert joined me for breakfast. We got up earlier than usual. We couldn't sleep because we were excited about going home. The morning dragged by. Ten o'clock came and went and nothing happened. We started getting nervous. Finally at 10:20 the phone rang. I could tell by his tone the news was not good. It was Mr. Gonzales from the Embassy. His first words were, "Lonnie, are you sitting down?" I sat down.

Mr. Gonzales began to break the news, "Now listen carefully, time is of the essence. *You are going to be charged!* You are going back to prison immediately, before noon at the latest. They will read to you what they are going to charge you with. A section of their law says, 'an act of remission or omission that is detrimental to the economic welfare of the sovereign country of Ghana'." I knew this was a catch-all law. If they couldn't find something specific to charge someone with, these words would let them do what they wanted. Gonzales told me the Ghanaian government felt they had to cover themselves since they had held me for seventeen days without charging me with something.

I repeated everything to Robert as I heard it from Gonzales. While I was talking he turned white as a sheet. I was afraid he was going to have a heart attack right in front of me! Gonzales said we had the right to an attorney. He told me to find one as soon as possible. He assured me that either he or his assistant would be standing beside us every step of the way. When the charges are read we had three options. We could plead guilty, not guilty or guilty with an explanation. He thought if we pled guilty with an explanation, we might get by with a fine or a short jail sentence or a combination of both. I didn't like these options. None of this sounded good to me. I hung up.

Robert and I discussed our situation. I mentioned the dinner we had the night before. Robert said if there was any time to call her, now was the time. I called her house. She wasn't home so I told her housekeeper who I was. I told her this was an emergency. I needed the Justice to call me. She called me in a few minutes. Her first words were, "Why didn't you tell me about this last night?"

I told her, "We thought it was all over, after all it was a social call and we didn't want to bother you with our problems. We had no idea it would come to this!"

She told us to sit tight, she would join us shortly. Robert and I waited a few minutes then went downstairs to the lobby to wait for her. About an hour after we talked on the phone she pulled up. She brought an attorney with her. The four of us talked outside the hotel where no one could hear us. She was not very encouraging. She told us, "I am a Justice. I cannot be seen with you. I will work behind the scenes to see what is going on. This is a kangaroo court not a justice court. It is totally separate from the regular court system. Any lawyer who appears before the tribunal will be disbarred. There will be no evidence presented and no opportunities for arguments."

The attorney she brought with her was her cousin. She went with us to the prison. I was relieved when the American Consulate showed up. Gonzales had promised us that he would be there but it felt good to see him. The Consulate had talked with the authorities before we got there. The authorities were hoping to get the situation taken care of quickly so they could take a Christmas break. They wanted everything decided within forty-eight hours. Talk about irony, "Let's put some Christians in jail so we can celebrate Christmas!"

We walked into the room. The room had four light fixtures but only one of them had a light bulb. The fluorescent bulb worked at either end but was dark in the middle. It was hard to make out faces because of the darkness. There were ten other Americans there who were being charges with crimes. They gave us books which had statements we were supposed to copy. Robert and I copied our statement. The Consulate was going to be our witness for the statement. We were pleading not guilty. This upset the Ghanaian authorities a lot. I found out that if we pleaded not guilty, they had to give us a hearing. They had no desire to go through a hearing. By the time we got finished copying our statements, having them properly witnessed and then filed with the court, it was starting to get dark outside. It became obvious that everything was going to be over that day.

They led us outside to a paddy wagon. They were taking us back to the prison where we were that first day. Our attorney and the American Consulate followed us in their car. When the paddy wagon pulled inside the prison gates, they stopped the Consulate's car. They were not allowed to go inside the walls. Once we got inside, they took us from the Paddy Wagon to a holding cell. Robert told me that he was familiar with everything we were doing. He had been through all of this before. I was not looking forward to stripping down to my shorts and putting my clothes in a box. The day that started with such hope was going down in flames.

We started getting ready to take our clothes off. Just then an officer walked inside the holding cell. He said, "We are going to release you to your respective consulates for the night. But you have to be back at nine in the morning for the tribunal."

Robert and I started praising the Lord right in the prison. It was almost like Paul and Silas in the Philippian jail. We really felt like we had escaped from the lion's mouth once again. Our attorney drove us back to the hotel. He told us he would meet us the next morning at the prison at 8:30. He promised to stand with us at the tribunal again. He told us to expect a sentence of up to six months with a $100,000 fine. They tribunal was allowed to keep the fines they levied for themselves. He also told us a different attorney had been found who had more experience with the tribunal. The new attorney wanted a four thousand dollar retainer to represent us.

I made a call to Tulsa. I told them everything about the day. I told Royce to deposit the money into a State Department account. The embassy would have access to the funds. I don't think anybody in Tulsa or Ghana got much sleep.

We got up early the next morning to meet with the new attorney. We drove to the American Embassy before we went to the prison. We heard the hearing was delayed. The Ghanaian authorities had decided to also charge our driver and the national director of our NGO. When the hearing started they brought the driver into the court room. It was their hope that the driver would testify against us. It was like they were looking for a way to make their case no matter what it took.

It seemed like every second dragged. Every tick of the clock took ten seconds and every minute was an eternity. They had originally scheduled everything to begin at nine but nothing was happening. When noon finally came we still hadn't seen anyone. Our attorney was afraid something had gone terribly wrong. We were sweating bullets through our dress clothes. The attorney began to go around and find out what was going on. He finally came back. He told us the head of the tribunal had gone downtown and wasn't coming back today. He told us to go back to the hotel. He assumed we would try again tomorrow at the same time. We were in the seventeenth day of our captivity. It seemed like it would never end. The American Consulate tried to cheer us up by taking us to lunch.

We got back to the hotel around two. Everything was in an uproar. The hotel staff told us two men had come to the hotel looking for us. When they told them we were not there, they became very angry. They wanted to get into our rooms. The staff told them we were at the tribunal. They told them they couldn't go in our rooms until we got back. This really upset them. They left but called back twice to see if we had come back to the hotel. They had just called a few minutes before we arrived. We went ahead to our rooms but it wasn't but a few minutes until the phone rang. They wanted to meet with us immediately!

We gave it a few minutes and walked down to the lobby. In walked two tall gruff Africans. One looked straight at me and said, "I am with Interpol!"

The other man said, "I am the chief of Immigration!"

We were not sure what was about to happen. We tried to steady ourselves for anything that might happen. We never expected to hear the next words we heard. In very angry gruff terms the two men nearly shouted at us. "We have news for you. *You have twenty-four hours to leave the country!*"

Robert and I said, "Praise the Lord!" I don't think the two Africans had ever heard those words before. It seemed to them that we must not have understood what was happening. They pulled a document out of their pocket officially informing us that we had twenty-four hours to leave the country beginning at noon. Since it was already three o'clock in the afternoon that meant we had twenty-one hours to leave the country.

I told them, "Wonderful! If there is a plane tonight I can be ready to go in fifteen minutes! But I don't have a passport!"

One of the tall guys told me he had my passport. I came back to him, "But where is my ticket?"

He told me he had a ticket for me. He was going to make certain we had reservations on a plane leaving the country. He said, "We will have you out of here by noon tomorrow."

Robert and I began to pepper them with questions. It seems the American Ambassador had met with the top officials of Ghana. He read them a list of sanctions the American government was prepared to put in place if the two of us were not released within two hours. We had been released while we were waiting for the tribunal to start. We didn't even know it! We were jumping up and down inside. We were going home!

We ran up to our rooms and called home. We nearly shouted the good news into the phone. I think they could have heard us across the Atlantic without a phone. A couple of hours later the hotel rang our rooms. The two big Africans were back. We were afraid something had changed. We were almost afraid to talk with them again. But we knew we had to talk to them.

We walked down the stairs to the lobby. The two men met us at the foot of the stairs like we were old friends. They patted us on the back and asked how we were doing? They told us that they had been told what great men we were. They heard about all of the great things we had done for Ghana! They wanted us to know that we were welcome to stay in Ghana for another week! They were afraid they would look bad for throwing two so important men out of the country. If we wanted to stay in Ghana they would like to invite us to their homes as their personal guests!

To say we were shocked would be an understatement. I told them how much we appreciated their kind words. But we had been away from home for a long time. Christmas was around the corner. We wanted to go home to our families as soon as we could. The two men sit down with us, asking about our families, our work, and everything else about us. Finally they said good-bye. When they left we weren't sure what was going on. We were sure there was some motive for what had just happened but I wasn't sure what it was.

On the last day the Ambassador came to see me again. He came into my room and said "Let's go out under the trees. You know your room has been bugged."

I told him I was aware of the bugs. When I came to my room I always said things for their benefit. So we walked out under the trees in front of the hotel so we could talk freely. The ambassador said to me, "I want to know who you are?"

I gave the answer I always gave, "I am Lonnie Rex from Tulsa, Oklahoma."

He looked at me and repeated his question. "I want to know WHO YOU ARE?"

I repeated the answer I had just given. "I am Lonnie Rex from Tulsa, Oklahoma."

Just like Jesus and Peter in John's gospel he asked me the third time. "I WANT TO KNOW WHO YOU ARE"?

I repeated for the third time the only answer I had. "I am Lonnie Rex from Tulsa, Oklahoma."

This time he didn't repeat his question but he answered it. "Now I know who you are. You are CIA. That is the official response of CIA agents, to say your name three times. I've been with the State Department and stationed in many countries of the world. But this is the only time I have had a teletype from the White House, signed by the White House, asking for an update on Lonnie Rex every day. What made it bad was our secure radio is about twenty miles outside of town on a small mountain. I have had to go out to that mountain every night to talk to the White House about Lonnie Rex. Now I know who you are. Now pack your suitcase you are going with me. They're going to let you out. But they're going to re-arrest you at the airport and take you to the penitentiary. They had found out what a big wig you are. They have a big fish. But if you will go with me, stay with me, hold on to me. Don't put your luggage on the plane. I will do that for you. I have you a ticket to the Ivory Coast. That will get you out of the country. You will have to make your way home from there."

The ambassador drove me to the airport. He walked me through the terminal and walked inside the plane, staying with me until I was seated. Once I was seated, he reached into his pocket and handed me my passport. He turned and walked away. He stood guard outside the door until the plane door was closed and we pulled away from the gate. He was making sure I was really gone. He wanted no last minute glitches.

The same day, they let all of my people go. Robert Boyd left the country about the same time I did. They let the driver and the printer go as well. I was really concerned about them because they didn't have an Embassy to work for them. Everyone got back to helping people get through the holidays.

It was about December 20th when I got to Ivory Coast. The only place I could get a ticket for was Nigeria. Then I got a ticket to Liberia. Then I finally got a ticket for New York. When I finally got my passport back, it was stamped in great big letters, *deported*.

When I finally got to New York, the Customs official glanced through my passport and saw that word, *deported*. He asked me if wanted to explain it. I was exhausted. All I wanted was to get home. So I looked at him and said, "Sir, haven't you heard. Ghana has deported all of the Seven Day Adventists and Mormons from the country!" He was so excited. He was a Mormon. He carried my bags for me to the next gate.

When I finally got home to Tulsa, I was a big celebrity. I didn't know, but the newspapers had been writing daily stories about the missionary arrested in Africa. Most of my staff and many of my friends were at the airport to greet me. I also didn't know that Royce had taken one hundred thousand dollars to the White House. Ghana was demanding a ransom for my release. But my friend and White House assistant Doug Wead wouldn't pay it. We eventually got our money back.

# ROMANIA

We did our best to answer every international disaster. I would personally go to supervise the distribution, so the supplies did not go to the local government or into the marketplace to be sold. We would send supplies by air shipment, boat or train, or even caravan, depending upon the continent we were working in. When we heard the Romanian dictator President Nicolai Ceausescu had been murdered and the people liberated. We wanted to give assistance to the starving people there. He had been the Communist dictator for over twenty years. Since we had an office in Europe we organized a collection campaign for food and clothing that filled five huge trucks. Royce called me.

As usual I wanted to be there to supervise the distribution. I immediately caught a plane, taking my travel agent friend with me. We landed in Dusseldorf, Germany. Our plan was to meet the caravan that was sent from Scotland. We were meeting them at the entrance city to Romania, Timisoara. I have a picture standing under a sign stretching across the highway at Timisoara. We had reserved a rental car. When we landed they told us they did not have the cheap rental car we had requested. They would have to give us a new Mercedes. We were so excited. It was fun driving across Germany on the autobahn at the high speed necessary to meet our caravan on time. When it came time to eat we would get off the autobahn, go into a small village and eat the local cuisine. We really enjoyed the great food.

By divine providence we met the caravan at Timisoara. We led the caravan from the border into the capital city of Bucharest. As we were driving, we would not see any farm houses along the highway. Then we would see a cluster of homes. Also we noticed there were no fences. We would drive many miles with no fences or homes, then a cluster would appear. This was disturbing to me because I had never seen anything like it in the world. When we got to the hotel I began to inquire. It was simple. This was a Communist country. All land was owned by the government. The communes, the cluster of homes, were the people who worked the land. No one owned anything. They were assigned their area to work.

We distributed the food at a church in Bucharest. Ceausescu gave his last speech as president on December 21. When he tried to address a crowd from his balcony they booed and jeered him. He tried to quiet the people, raising his hands and promising them more money. But nothing he said helped. The revolution had started. The next day he tried again to give a speech. This time the people threw rocks and anything else they could grab.

When Ceausescu ran back into the building the people gave chase. They got within a few feet of him in an elevator. He escaped by helicopter. They got away to one of their other homes but soon the people found them there. They escaped again by helicopter but by then the army had changed sides. On Christmas Eve they forced the helicopter to land in a field where Nicolai and his wife Elena were arrested. Ceausescu and his wife were executed on Christmas day of 1989. They were convicted in a court of genocide and the illegal gathering of wealth. They were immediately taken outside with their hands behind their back and shot by an elite group of paratroopers. He went from being the leader of the country to being executed for abuse of power in five days.

We were there within ten days or so of their liberation distributing food. I will always remember the Christians in the church where we distributed the food saying it was appropriate that Ceausescu was executed on Christmas Day because he had robbed them of Christmas for so many years. They really hated him because he was a terrible dictator.

# BANGLADESH

It was indeed a blessed day when I met you in Thailand in 1975 when you shared with me your lifelong compassion for the poorest of the poor – next door and around the world! It was my privilege to be involved with your work in Asia – especially in Bangladesh and in Thailand – and oversee your work there for a few years! In the kaleidoscope of my mind run many fond memories of being with you in many places of the world with many different people and in many different situations. I treasure them all fondly. The brotherly love you showed to me and all on-the-spot relief workers is an example to us all. We praise God for you and your service to the poor and the needy in His Name!

—Dulal Borpujari – Bangkok, Thailand

Soon after gaining their independence from India, there was a tsunami in Bangladesh. When we arrived at Dhaka, the capital, the President met with the leaders of NGOs who had come from all over the world to help with the situation. All of the other NGOs wanted to stay close to the capital. The President of Bangladesh said if we would go where no one else wanted to go, he would give us his helicopter to get there. So we loaded his helicopter but we traveled to a place that later took us nine hours by car and three ferries to get there. We put up a huge tent and made a makeshift hospital. We were the largest hospital within two hundred square miles.

The land where the tent was erected was owned by the brother of the Bangladesh Minister of the Interior. They begged us to build a hospital. Later he sold us five acres for the hospital.

The first thing the doctors did was pull bodies from the tops of the trees. We had to create a makeshift morgue. The Muslims buried their dead the same day they die. The village leaders in the area recruited help to dig the graves.

There were no utility services of any kind where the hospital tent was erected. The first thing we did was dig a pond to collect rain water. We had to boil the water but at least we had some. Hygiene was a problem. The people would bathe in the ponds where the animals also bathed and drank. We had to teach the people basic hygiene. We taught the nursing mothers to clean themselves with boiled water because they were transferring disease from their dirty breasts to their infants. We had to teach them to wash their babies in boiled water. This eliminated many of the health questions that brought people to the doctor. We taught the men to wash themselves as well. We had women teach women and men teach men.

Men and women had to be treated at different times because of the Muslim teachings of the separation of men and women. So, women would come to the clinic on Mondays, the men would come on Tuesdays, and Wednesday was the day for the children. On Thursday women and children were seen at the clinic. Friday was also a children's day.

One of the amazing things I learned was that although this was a strict Muslim country, venereal disease was rampart. We were constantly bringing in antibiotics to treat the problem. One night I heard a knock on my door. Although I couldn't talk to the man he let me know he needed to come in. Men in Bangladesh wear a type of skirt called a *lungi*. It ties around the top. When the man got inside, since he couldn't talk to me he just acted. He untied his *lungi*. It fell to the floor. What I saw was the worst thing I had ever seen. He had open sores and scabs from his belly button to his knees. His private area was one big bloody scab.

It just so happened that I had some antibiotics in the room with me. I gave him four pills. I drew a clock and pointed to the times he was supposed to take the additional drugs. Then I told him he had to come back tomorrow to get more drugs. The doctors had told me that it took four pills a day for ten days to clear up venereal disease. I made him come back because I knew if I gave him forty pills he would either sell them or take them all in a short time. This seemed the best because I couldn't communicate with him.

I was happy to see him every day for the next ten days. He would knock on my door at night. He would walk in, drop his skirt, and I would give him the drugs. By the end of the time, I knew for certain he was clean.

The next time I came back, he had spread the word far and wide. I didn't get any sleep for ten days. I tried to get them to go to the local doctors. We had hired Muslim doctors. But they wouldn't go because they didn't want people in the village to know they had this disease. So I began teaching classes on venereal disease. I would tell them that I had a miracle drug from America that would cure the problem. But I would also tell them that if they didn't get the problems treated, they would die. To get treatment, they had to tell me where they had been. Prostitution was common. To get treatment they also had to bring their wife to the clinic. We knew she had been infected. If she wasn't treated they would just pass the disease back and forth. So they came in for treatment. But they would only come at night. They would only come to my room. I became the VD room!

I had two ladies on my staff. Ladies who wanted to go to Bangladesh with me. I tried to tell them about the problem. These were married women with sons. I told them you are not going to see anything you haven't seen before, but you are going to see something you have never seen before. One night about two o'clock, I called them to come to my room. I had the badly infected man there. I told him I had brought staff from the States to help me. To preserve his modesty I put a pillow case over his head. They quietly walked in. He dropped his skirt and I thought the ladies were going to faint. They had seen my pictures but they didn't believe it until they saw it with their own eyes. I told them, "This is why we are here."

Because of all of this, I called in the government health police. The men were all going to a prostitution house in a village about five miles away. The government came in and arrested the women and took them to a place where they could be treated for the disease. We cleaned up the VD in the area but it took about a year.

They began to build the hospital a few months after the tent was erected. It was obvious the need was much greater than the tsunami. The outside wall was wood. Although the wood was expensive, it was still cheaper than brick and there were no brick layers in the area. The inside walls were woven mats. St. Frances Hospital in Tulsa gave us all of our beds, equipment, bed pans, everything else. We were the most fully equipped hospital in Bangladesh including X-ray equipment. Early every morning, three to five hundred people would line up under the trees outside of the hospital. They were waiting for dawn so they could be treated. They had all walked there. If we needed someone to stay over to be treated again the next day, they would sleep under the trees. We only had about twenty-eight beds for the most critical patients. We would also keep new mothers and their infants overnight.

To keep the operating rooms sterile, there were no windows. We only had electricity between eight and ten at night. Surgeries were performed by flashlight. We couldn't use generators because we couldn't bring in the fuel. We were in the jungle. Bangladesh is a Moslem country. If we had used the word Christian, the people would not have come. When we got ready to open the permanent hospital, I formed a committee of local people. They told me that because they were Moslem, the hospital could not be open on Saturday. Out of respect for their religion, I agreed. But I told them that this was a Christian hospital, so it would be closed on Sunday in respect for our faith. We were closed on Saturday to honor the Moslems and on Sunday to honor Christ.

Everyone agreed the hospital would deal with true emergencies as necessary. The government registered the hospital as the Lonnie Rex Hospital.

Lonnie in Bangladesh

Across the road, a school was built. When we first erected the original tent hospital it was a few miles to the nearest village. But over time a small village grew around us. There was a marketplace built where people could trade and sell things. Eventually the village elders built a school. We gave them a large donation to help with the construction. They named the school the Betty Rex School. Betty became well known in the community.

During this time Betty had blonde hair. I got her a rickshaw with her name on the back. I hired a rickshaw driver. On the days when the men were at the clinic, she would go out into the villages and talk with the women. She would talk with them about their babies and children. She was loved for miles around because she came to their homes and played with their children. When she saw a child in need of attention, she would bring it to the clinic or have a doctor go to the home. Her rickshaw is still there. She still sends a Christmas gift to her driver.

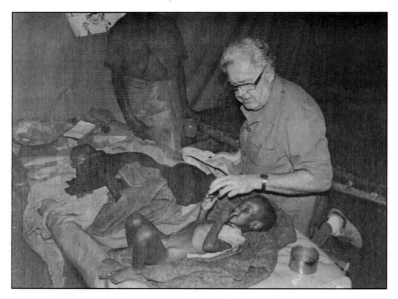

Lonnie with baby in Bangladesh

Betty and I became very well known in that area. We bought an old Range Rover to get us from Dhaka to the hospital. There wasn't an airport and we didn't have a helicopter. The Range Rover eventually died after it had three hundred thousand miles on it. We would leave Dhaka around six in the morning and get to the hospital about three or four in the afternoon. The roads would get worse and worse as we went into the jungle. We had to use three ferries. The last thirty miles or so was just a dirt road. It was always muddy because it is always raining there. When we got within a quarter of a mile or so from the hospital we had to stop because of the crowd around the hospital. When word got out there would be two thousand people or more there to greet us. I would walk that last distance to greet and touch the people. It would generally take an hour to walk that final five hundred yards.

Dhaka was about ninety miles from the hospital. It took us to so long to get to the hospital because of the road conditions. The Japanese had built a new hotel there in Dhaka. I always stayed in the Sheraton when I was in Dhaka because they had a restaurant which served American style food. But the staff wanted me to stay in the new Japanese hotel. I stayed there but I didn't like their food. At lunch time I would get a rickshaw and go down to the Sheraton to eat. One day after lunch I was coming back to the hotel in my rickshaw when I noticed a big commotion in the street. The rickshaw driver stopped but I told him to take me to the hotel. He walked around the crowd and got me to the door of the hotel.

I got out, paid and tipped the driver. While I was standing there a big black limousine drove up behind me. I walked over to the car. Then I noticed that most of the hotel staff was standing in a straight line from the front door to the desk. They pushed me into their receiving line. Out of the limo stepped the president of Bangladesh. He was coming to dedicate the new Japanese hotel. So I start to shake hands. Soon the President walked up behind me and said, "Who are you?"

I told him, "I am Lonnie Rex from Tulsa, Oklahoma. I am trying to get to my room."

He told me that he was the President of Bangladesh. He thought that was so funny that I was in the receiving line. He asked me to keep walking and go inside with him to dedicate the hotel. I did. When we got finished, he told me I better go upstairs to my room before they find out who I really am.

Royce managed our office in Scotland for several years. There he met Dan Wooding, who was a British journalist and the son of missionaries to Africa. He wrote a story about our office in Scotland. Through this article he and Royce became friends. He asked what we were doing around the world. He became so interested that we sent him around the world. We sent him to Bangladesh. He wrote a story with the headline, *The Hospital No One Would Build.* That gave us tremendous publicity in the UK and in Europe.

The ministry in Bangladesh impacted Betty and I more personally than any other ministry we had in the whole world. The security guard for the hospital, Mr. Uddin, became our friend. We would go to visit him and his family in their little home. They had a nice little home. You would walk into what we would call their living room. There was a door with a curtain on it. Everyone in the first room were men. There were no windows, just shutters. But out of every opening in the hut there would be twenty guys looking in.

I ask Mr. Uddin where his wife was? He called loudly and this sweet little woman walked through the door. I immediately liked her, so I grabbed her and kissed her on the cheek. Betty followed my lead and did the same. Suddenly there were gasps from the crowd looking through the windows. She obviously was taken aback. We knew we had done something culturally amiss. They had a young adult son who was there. I asked about his wife. She walks in and Betty and I repeat the same display of affection we had with her mother-in-law. We didn't know we had humiliated both of them in front of their Muslim neighbors. The next time we came to visit the hospital, the guard and his son invited us back to their home. They said their wives wanted us to come back and give them a kiss!

Every year in Bangladesh, they have a lottery to win a visa to the United States. Fifty thousand people can win a Green card to come to the United States. Mr. Uddin's son was entered and he won! Mr. Uddin begged me to help his son come to America. Because he had been so faithful to work at the hospital, I couldn't say no. He asked me to take him to my house and make him a houseboy. We weren't going to make him a houseboy, but we did bring him to the United States.

We didn't know it, but he had only attended school one day in his life. School wasn't for him. But he did have a trade. He was the local gambler. He had never worked a more normal job in his life. He also smoked heavily, which we didn't know until he landed in Tulsa. It was July when he landed. He wore a wool suit

202

someone had bought him just for the trip. The only other clothes he had with him was the lungi or skirt he wore in Bangladesh. I told him he had to smoke outside. After a few days that wasn't working, so I told him he had to stop smoking altogether. I told him if he didn't stop smoking we would send him back. It almost killed him but he stopped.

The next weekend, my kids took him to the local Bell's amusement park. He had never seen anything like this. They got him on the roller coaster. He was so scared, he wet himself. When they got him home, I had to help him in the shower. He had never seen an American shower before. I had to show him how to mix the hot and cold faucets so he wouldn't freeze of scald himself. It took a while. He kept his skirt on because he always bathed in streams and ponds before with others around. They always kept their clothes on. But over time his clothes still began to smell. But he began to learn some English. I was able to teach him that in the shower he could shut the door and have total privacy. He could take all of his clothes off when he bathed.

We had a housekeeper at the time. Between her and Betty, he began to learn some English. But there was still a cultural clash. Women do not give orders to men in Bangladesh. He rebelled against everything they said. Later, when he learned more English, he said to me, "Poppa, every night I cried myself to sleep. Betty was so cruel. I was so lonesome. I didn't think anyone liked me."

I decided he needed to get out of the house. I got him a job with a friend of mine. He rebuilt cars. They could teach him to sand. He didn't need a lot of English for that. I decided I wasn't going to be a taxi for him. I got him a bus pass. I went to the bus stop with him. The bus went downtown. I showed him how to change buses. I showed him how to get to work and how to get home. This scared him to death. This was a kid from a small Bangladesh village riding a bus in a major American city. He worked there for several months. They liked him.

But there was a restaurant a few blocks from the house. They needed a dishwasher. In Bangladesh that was woman's work. But it paid more money and he understood money. He started working there because it paid more and he didn't have to ride the bus. But a little further down was another restaurant. They offered him a job as a waiter. This restaurant was across the street from Oral Roberts University. They catered to students and faculty from there. At first he didn't know how to write their orders, and he would just go to the kitchen and tell them what they wanted. But they worked with him. During this time I hired him a tutor who taught him more English using the menu to practice. He eventually became the head waiter.

Later he went to work at the Sheridan Hotel as the head waiter there. About this time, he bought his first car and Betty taught him how to drive. That was a real experience all by itself. He had a wife and three children in Bangladesh. He was sending money back to care for them. It took us ten years of filling out papers, but they were finally able to come to the United States.

One of his friends from Bangladesh had purchased a convenience store. It was in a good location. The night manager had been killed in a robbery, so he had purchased it cheap. They had not been able to find people to work there. About that time they began to crack down on illegal immigrants. His buddy was not a legal immigrant so he fled to Canada. So he was left with the convenience store. Ten years after he immigrated to the United States, he owns three convenience stores, lives in a half million dollar home, drives a Lexus and his son drives a sports car.

He now sponsors people back home. He travels back and forth at least once a year. He helps people there. Betty and I consider him and his wife to be our Bangladesh kids, and his kids our grandkids. They come to our home during the holidays. He has created the American dream.

# THAILAND — HONG KONG — ASIA

Giving utmost concern to the poor and the underprivileged is the clamor of the hour today in order to minimize, if not, eradicate the countless number of suffering humanity in our midst. If all civic organizations only possess the same noble objectives as yours, certainly, our world will be a happy and a prosperous place to live in.

—Osmundo G. Rama M.D.
Republic of the Philippines – Province of Cebu

Back in the 1970s, Hong Kong was so overcrowded with refugees that they did not have land to build schools. Their schools were on the rooftops of their skyscrapers. We sponsored the rooftop schools.

During the Vietnamese boat people were escaping from Vietnam, we bought an old tug of a boat. It had to be repaired every time it came in to keep it chugging. We partnered with Food for the Hungry, led by Larry Ward, we picked up the boat people and brought them into the refugee camp in Hong Kong. For many years we received thank you notes from Vietnamese people who finally made it to the United States.

A few years ago I was introduced by TL Osborn in a banquet in Houston, Texas. Sitting at an adjoining table were two Vietnamese pastors of the largest Vietnamese Baptist churches in Houston. One jumped up and knelt at my chair. He told me his mother and nine children escaped from Communist Vietnam on three small boats and rafts. They did not know if their family would ever be reunited. They did make their way to the United States and were adopted by a Lutheran Church in Wisconsin who housed and educated the entire family. Three of the brothers are pastors today.

I immediately told him about our tug who picked up refugees. I said, "My tug, pick your momma and nine children up. I cannot prove that nor can you disprove it. Therefore, I adopt you today. He and his family have become very close friends the last few years.

In fact, last Christmas at noon, we had dinner with his mother and several of their children and grandchildren. Since he had married a Vietnamese wife from Brazil, at three o'clock we went to the Brazilian side of the family and had another feast. At six o'clock we went to another Vietnamese, Dr. Victoria Bryant, who also left Vietnam on a small boat and was adopted by a family in Houston. She is now a doctor of Pharmacy and president of the Vietnamese Chamber of Commerce. Her wonderful husband is Dr. Ron Bryant who is head of all wound clinics for the famous Herman Memorial Hospitals. We had another Vietnamese feast and met more family members. In fact we grazed all day.

In Thailand, we ran across a school led by the daughter of a general of the Air Force. He was a Buddhist but his daughter and her husband were Christians. They started a Christian school and we supported them. We found an individual sponsor for each student in the school. The sponsor provided them with all of their books and school supplies. It was about forty miles outside of Bangkok. It became the largest and most respected school in the area. We had a strong chapel service every day. They were Pentecostal and the chapel service reflected that. The school made a strong stand for Christ in that area.

Because of her father's position in the government, we had protection. We needed the protection because it was the law that every school had to have a Buddha in every classroom. She was adamant there would be no Buddha in the classrooms. Every year when someone came to accredit the school, there was a fight over this. They would try to close the school down. The fight would go all the way to the top.

We also supported a leper village in Thailand for many years. We provided food and shelter to everyone in the village. There was a school for the children to attend with a teacher we sponsored. We also built a church and sponsored the pastor.

Our orphanage in Cebu City, Philippines, had a music director who was extraordinary. They sang for me once while I was there on a visit. They thought they were doing this just for our visit. It would be a one-time thing. I was so impressed with the director and so impressed with the children that I suggested we augment it, put him on salary, have regular rehearsals, and bring them to America. We had a lady on staff who called our friends and sponsors, arranged a stop every hundred miles or so.

We landed in Los Angeles and worked our way back to Tulsa. We had a series of concerts in Los Angeles. The CEO of Disney, Michael Eisner had daughters who attended a private school hosted by a Pentecostal church. The school director announced the student body that the Filipino choir was coming to sing. They told their father. He called the school director. Told the director if the choir would sing at Disneyland, he would make arrangements for them to spend the day at the park for free. The kids were thrilled. It was a privilege for the kids to sing for that crowd. It was also very generous of Michael Eisner to allow these kids, raised in poverty, to have that experience.

Then we worked our way to the East Coast, including New York City. We did this twice. It was such a hit for us. Every night we would get sponsors for orphans. The kids would stay in the homes of the parishioners. We would place two little boys or two little girls in a home. People fell in love with the kids. People became their sponsors. They would send them Christmas gifts, birthday gifts and other things.

# THE WORK CONTINUES

When I retired in 1997, I was sure the end of my life was not far ahead. My family and friends were all encouraging me to retire. I was having serious heart problems which had to have my immediate focus. A few days after my retirement celebration, I entered the hospital for triple bypass surgery. I thought I would never be the same again. The truth was I wasn't. I was starting the next chapter of my life. This was a chapter where instead of working for one organization, I would work for the Church around the world.

I spent about six weeks recovering from the surgery where the doctors cracked my chest. But even during those few weeks, my telephone never stopped ringing. In the beginning, the calls were to ask about my health. But the conversations moved from, "How's he doing", to "Is he able to talk" and then "Could I talk with Lonnie"? As I began to feel better I would talk on the telephone to friends around the world.

In the beginning they would ask me for advice and direction on where they should go. But soon they were asking me to take a more formal role in their organizations. As of 2013, I serve on the boards of ten humanitarian organizations in four countries. I am assisting those organizations by referring them to several of my contacts with whom I have maintained relationships over the last forty years. I have shared with them contacts where they can obtain food and other supplies that can help people around the world.

I take these organizations seriously. I am not a figurehead member where they place my name on a letterhead to boost my ego and help the prestige of the organization. I attend meetings, make and take telephone calls and send emails. I ask questions and give my best advice and direction. I must say I am surprised that I received these phone calls in the beginning but now I also see it as a part of the calling of God on my life in the latter part of my life. I have believed all of my life that if God opens a door I should walk through it. God has opened doors in my life.

One of the doors that opened which surprised me was the door to Russia. I had relationships with many high ranking officials in that country. Some of these people were not high officials when I met them the first time, but over time they had grown into high positions. One of these people was Vladimir Putin. I met him back in the 1980s when he was assigned to me as a KGB agent. Every American who entered the old Soviet Union was assigned a KGB agent. Their job was to monitor everything I did and make sure I didn't go where I wasn't supposed to go or do what I shouldn't do.

It wasn't a secret that Putin was assigned to me. He was around me everywhere I went. When I walked out of a hotel room in the morning he would be nearby. When I went into my room and night he would be close by. I am sure someone else monitored my room at night, making sure I didn't leave or receive visitors I shouldn't. But Putin was the guy around the most.

On the last day of 1999 Vladimir Putin became acting president of Russia. Boris Yeltsin had resigned unexpectedly so Putin was sworn into the position. Within a few weeks an election was held. Putin was elected to a full four year term as President of Russia. He was to be sworn in on May 7, 2000. Shortly after his election, Betty and I received an invitation to attend the inauguration in Moscow.

We flew on Aeroflot Airlines in a direct flight from Chicago to Moscow. The flight was a short twelve hour flight. We stayed at the National Hotel, across the street from the Kremlin. We were the guests of the Russian government for ten days. I knew several of the high ranking officials of the government.

One evening, I received a call from Stroven Egor Semenovich, chairman of the Russian Senate. He asked for Betty and me to meet him in the lobby of the hotel at seven the next morning. Since we were their guests, I thought it would be rude to not accept their invitation.

Even though it was nearly the middle of May it was still cool when we stepped outside. Spring and summer are short and not nearly as hot as the Oklahoma summers we had when I was a child. He had a limousine for us. They drove us to the edge of Moscow to a small airport. We boarded a small plane which took us to one of the Great Russian national forest. By this time it was getting close to lunch time. Betty and I were a little hungry since we had breakfast so early but we didn't say anything. We were taken to a very nice resort. Before the fall of communism it was reserved for the party elite.

We were escorted into a banquet room when I was shocked. President Smenovich had prepared a celebration for my birthday! In all of the inaugural festivities I had forgotten. It was May 11, my 73rd birthday. Some of the local party leaders were present. I received some very nice gifts. Many of them had heard how I helped raise money for the widows and orphans of the Afghanistan War. They had also heard about my role in helping the Russians avoid a potato famine. It also didn't hurt that I was friends with President Putin. After the party we were flown back to Moscow.

The next time I came back to Russia I came with my grandson. That was the trip where I was knighted after the order of Malta. That has already been covered, but by that time I knew I wasn't living like a retired man. But my experiences with the nation of Russia were not over.

One morning in 2011, I received a call from a friend who worked for Phillips Oil Company in Bartlesville, Oklahoma.

He said he was coming through Houston for some business and wanted to get together. When he got to town we met together for a soft drink. We had a good time together. I entertained him with some of my stories. I included some about my trips to Russia.

That night he had dinner with someone from the Russian-American Federation. He began to recount the stories I had told him about Russia. As he told the stories he finally mentioned me by name. When he did that, their eyes lit up. They immediately recognized my name. They told to him, "Dr. Lonnie Rex is a very well-known name in Russia. Do you have his telephone number? We would love to do a story about him for our Russian-American Federation magazine." He gave them my phone number. They called me straight from the dinner table.

They told me they were leaving Houston the next morning for Tulsa. They were attending the graduation ceremony at ORU. They asked me to meet them at 7:00 the next morning for an interview for their magazine. When we sat down at the table they began to tell me my own stories about Russia! They had heard many of the legends of Lonnie Rex. We talked for over two hours. At the end of our time they asked me to become a member of the board of their organization.

In 2012 I got a call from the Russian consulate in Houston. They asked me to join them at a dinner to honor NASA. They were raising money to place statues of the first American Astronaut and the first Russian Cosmonaut on the grounds of NASA. I met some of my friends from the Russian-American Federation. It seems like I will be connected to Russia for the rest of my life.

Betty and I still have a burning passion to see the Lonnie R. Rex Hospital and the Betty Rex School rebuilt in Bangladesh. We built both of those in the early 1970s. The story has been told earlier. The facilities were built about two and a half miles from the Muhuri River. This river is the geographic dividing line between Bangladesh and India. A typhoon came through and changed the course of the river. The new course destroyed both facilities and swept them down the river. This hospital served everyone within two hundred square miles. It had served as a beacon of hope for tens of thousands of people for well over twenty years. The school had served hundreds of children over the years. It had given them hope for their lives. Now all of this is gone.

It is my hope to rebuild the hospital and school. I have a pledge of a million dollars to purchase the land for the facilities. The former Bangladesh ambassador to Russia has agreed to be the new director of the Lonnie Rex Hospital. I expect to travel to Bangladesh in the fall of 2013 to begin the process of purchasing the land. I will also obtain the permits to build the new facilities. I hope to raise the money to complete the project before 2015. I believe God has given me until I am 90 to do his work. That gives me through 2017 to get the job done.

I love to travel and go whenever I can. I replaced Oral Roberts on the board of the Oral Roberts Evangelistic Association when Oral passed away. Richard invited me to be a part of a crusade. One morning I received a call asking me to come down to the lobby. What I didn't know was Richard Roberts got the same call I did.

When we got down to the lobby there were two very distinguished black men there to greet us. One of them I already knew. He was from San Antonio. He served on the board of the Oral Roberts Evangelistic Association with Richard and me. He reached out to us and shook our hand. He said, "I want you to meet the half-brothers of President Barack Obama." The men were very gracious and kind to us. We had a nice time chatting with them. I invited them to attend the crusade. They came to the meeting. One of them went forward to the healing line. As we talked with them we finally determined they were actually step-brothers of President Obama. His father had married their mother but he was never their father.

I still live for the adventures with God. As I grow older, I see the hand of God on my life. To have been a small boy in

Oklahoma with polio, no one would have ever believed I could go the places and do the things I have done. For God to have opened the door to work with some of the greatest evangelists of the 20th century has been amazing. To have met with presidents, prime ministers, queens and kings, is one the honors of life.

I must say, one of the highlights of my life was the audience with Pope John Paul II. I love great art. The art in the summer Vatican is beyond description. Some of the greatest pieces of art in world hang in the hallways of the summer Vatican. It seems a shame for such beautiful pieces of art to be seen by so few people.

One of the proverbs of my life has been, I don't ask God for money, I ask him for ideas. God has been faithful. I played a role in reaching tens of thousands of people through the ministries of Oral Roberts, TL Osborn and Billy James Hargis, plus others. I raised millions of dollars, added many television and radio stations to expand their ministries to reach the United States and the world.

God gave me a heart to help meet the needs of people. I will never forget going to TL Osborn to get him to help orphans in Haiti. He told me words that changed my life. "You do what God tells you to do and I will do what God tells me to do." I immediately began to plan to do whatever it took to help meet those needs. God open the doors. Thousands of children were fed. Leper colonies in Asia and Africa were cared for. Millions of pounds of food have been distributed in nations around the world. God has been with me every day. If I could share a few words with those who come after me, those words would be, "God is faithful."

# OBSERVATIONS

Meeting and working with Dr. Lonnie R. Rex has been one of the greatest experiences in my life. The time I have spent with him has changed my life forever. Watching him talk with people from around the country is amazing. The first time I went to his home I spent nearly four days with him. I recorded nearly sixty hours of interviews with him during those days. It seems nearly impossible to do that much until you find out that Lonnie does not sleep very much.

If I was to describe Lonnie Rex in a few words it would be, "Dr. Lonnie R. Rex is a Matthew 25 man. He lives those verses more than any other man in the world. Those words drive him with a passion that few people in the world understand."

For those who have forgotten these are some of the words from Matthew 25. Matthew 25:34-40

> Then the King will say to those on his right, 'Come, you who are blessed by my Father; take your inheritance, the kingdom prepared for you since the creation of the world. 35 For I was hungry and you gave me something to eat, I was thirsty and you gave me something to drink, I was a stranger and you invited me in, 36 I needed clothes and you clothed me, I was sick and you looked after me, I was in prison and you came to visit me.' 37 "Then the righteous will answer him, 'Lord, when did we see you hungry and feed you, or thirsty and give you something to drink? 38 When did we see you a stranger and invite you in, or

> needing clothes and clothe you? 39 When did we see you
> sick or in prison and go to visit you?' 40 "The King will
> reply, 'I tell you the truth, whatever you did for one of the
> least of these brothers of mine, you did for me.' (NIV)

Lonnie Rex is a man who has reached out to the least for over a half century. The least can be hundreds of orphans, who need someone to feed them, clothe, educate and put a roof over their head. Lonnie has been there for thousands of children around the world. But the least may also be someone nationally and internationally recognized who is going through a crisis in their life or ministry. Every time I go to Lonnie's house, between interviews he takes calls from Christian leaders from around the country. Nearly every Christian leader who has been involved in a personal or ministry scandal in the last quarter century, Lonnie has been the go-to guy.

Some would dispute that televangelists can be the least of these, but Lonnie doesn't question the person, he seeks to resolve the problem. He is truly a man who sees problems as opportunities. He resolves problems of any type at any place in the world. If the problem is the lack of a car in India, he walks into the office of the Minister of Transportation to cut all of the red tape. When the waiting list is seven years, it suddenly becomes a few hours. When Mother Teresa needs a right hand drive ambulance to pick up corpses in the streets of Calcutta, Lonnie solves the problem. Lonnie goes beyond the verses of Matthew 25; he serves those who are gone on.

So many ministries are focused on what impact things will make on them. They seem to place the emphasis on themselves. Whenever there is a photo opportunity they will be found near the front. Many of these people never found a television camera they didn't like. They will feed a hundred children and spend two hundred hours on television taking credit for it. They have a crusade for a few hours and repeat the service for donations as many times as possible.

Lonnie is the opposite. He has appeared on television many times, but he uses every opportunity to tell about the needs of his *kids*. He will tell of the leper villages where a moped is needed to take supplies. He will tell of traveling to the furthest islands in the perimeter of the Philippines or Indonesia. He goes where no one else is willing to go. He does not seek headlines but he has accomplished things the world should hear from the housetops.

The first time I was in his home a major Christian leader was going through a very difficult time. Lonnie would take his calls several times a day. Lonnie did not give him tell him what to do. But he was the wise father who cared and heard his pain. Sometimes Lonnie would ask to have privacy and other times he would just talk. There were times when you realized this was not the same person he talked with earlier. He was juggling the different issues of more than one ministry. Lonnie Rex has become the wise counselor to the Christian world.

Lonnie Rex knows more about the church in the latter half of the 20$^{th}$ century than anyone else in the world. All of Lonnie's knowledge is first hand. It just goes on and on. I would sit in his office at his home and ask him about the greatest ministries of the 20$^{th}$ century. There are some gaps but very few. He has stories about Billy Graham and Pope John Paul II. He met the leaders of many of the branches of the Orthodox Church as well as the leaders of the Coptic Churches of North Africa. He has known every leader of the Assembly of God and International Pentecostal Holiness Church for over fifty years. He has been friends with Charles Stanley for nearly forty years. He knows the inside of several ministries. He has appeared several times on both PTL and TBN. He bought a television station from Jim Bakker and sold it to Paul Crouch. He was a co-host of a daily television program with Ernest Angley. There is no one else on planet earth who can speak of all of these people plus many others on a first hand basis.

Another thing which touches you is how Lonnie has never met a situation where he encountered fear. Lonnie has walked into the office of the Minister of Transportation in India. He needed a car so he went to the top. When he couldn't get an ambulance released to take to a hospital in Africa, he again walked into the office of the top transportation official in the country. When he has a problem he goes to the top official he can find.

Lonnie is a gem of the Christian world. Like a diamond he was created by walking through the fire of service to the King. My goal for the rest of his life is to help him spread the word about the greatness of our God. When you listen to Lonnie talk about the many times when the Lord has guided him through some of the most treacherous places on earth. It is impossible to hear his stories without believing God can do anything.

Lonnie needs to be telling his stories everywhere to everyone. I wish young people would listen to Lonnie tell them to do grand things for God. In the 21st century many churches have moved to a structured service to bring the masses in and out in a timely manner. Lonnie talks about moving in God's timing to do God's bidding.

—Richard Young